Godly Man

MEN as Leaders

Kurt Krueger

D0167368

CPH
SAINT LOUIS

Contents

Series editors: Thomas J. Doyle and Rodney L. Rathmann
This publication is also available in braille and in large print for the visually impaired. Write to Library for the Blind, 1333 S. Kirkwood Road, St. Louis, MO 63122-7295 or call 1-800-433-3954. Unless otherwise indicated, scripture quotations are taken from THE HOLY BIBLE: NEW INTERNATIONAL VERSION®. NIV®. Copyright © 1973, 1978, 1984 by International Bible Society. Used by permission of Zondervan Publishing House. All rights reserved. Verses taken from THE LIVING BIBLE are copyright © 1971 by Tyndale House Publishers, Wheaton, IL. Used by permission. Excerpt on pp. 8–9 from SERVANT LEADERSHIP by Robert K. Greenleaf, © 1977 by Robert K. Greenleaf; © 1991 by The Robert K. Greenleaf Center. Used by permission of Paulist Press. Excerpts on pp. 13–14, 24–25, 45–48, 49–50, 50–52, and 77–83 taken from **The Book of God** by Walter Wangerin, Jr. Copyright © 1995 by Walter Wangerin, Jr. Used by permission of Zondervan Publishing House. Excerpts on pp. 18–19 and 20 reprinted from THEY CALL ME COACH by John Wooden, © 1988. Used with permission of NTC/Contemporary Publishing Group, Inc. Excerpt on p. 19 reprinted from WOODEN: A LIFETIME OF OBSERVATIONS & REFLECTIONS ON AND OFF THE COURT by John Wooden, © 1977. Used by permission of NTC/Contemporary Publishing Group, Inc. Excerpt on pp. 21–22 from pages 125—28 from the book titled *On Solid Ground* by Tom Osborne, © 1996 by Nebraska Book Company. Excerpt on p. 31 from LINCOLN ON LEADERSHIP by Donald T. Phillips II. By permission of Warner Books. Excerpts on pp. 57 and 58–60 from BLACK LIKE ME by John Howard Griffin. Copyright © 1961 by John Howard Griffin, rnwd 1989 by Elizabeth Griffi-Bonazzi, Susan Griffin-Campbell, J. H. Griffin, Jr., Greg Griffin, Amanda Griffin-Sanderson. Used by permission of Dutton Signet, a division of Penguin Putnam, Inc. Excerpt on pp. 71–73 © 1998 Time Inc. Reprinted by permission.

INTRODUCTION

The Godly Man Series

In his letter to the recently established Christian church at Philippi, the apostle Paul likened the Christian life to a race. Paul wrote, "Forgetting what is behind and straining toward what is ahead, I press on toward the goal to win the prize for which God has called me heavenward in Christ Jesus" (Philippians 3:13–14).

Each of us who by faith claims Jesus as Lord and Savior has God's permission and His power to forget "what is behind." Over two thousand years ago, Jesus came to earth, true God, Son of the eternal Father, and yet true man. Conceived by the Holy Spirit and born of the Virgin Mary, Jesus grew as a boy—through childhood and adolescence—to become a mature man. He endured all the temptations and struggles every man has faced and yet committed no sin of thought, word, or action (Hebrews 4:14–15). According to His Father's plan, He suffered and died on the cross as our substitute, taking our sins upon Himself. We can forget our sins because Jesus' love has overcome our past. He has won the victory over our sins and the constraining, handicapping power of the devil. Jesus showed Himself Lord over sin, death, and the devil when He rose from the dead on Easter morning. We who believe in the crucified, risen, and ascended Savior are made new men by the same Holy Spirit who brought us to faith. As God's Spirit gives us new desires and a new set of goals and priorities, He changes us through the Word of God—the Gospel—so that we come to know God's love and the outpouring of His grace in mighty ways, and grow in our relationship with our Father in heaven. By inspiration of the Holy Spirit, long ago the psalmist wrote the following insight into God and His nature, "His pleasure is not in the strength of the horse, nor His delight in the legs of a man; the LORD delights in those who fear Him, who put their hope in His unfailing love" (Psalm 147:10–11).

As we run life's race, our heavenly Father invites us to find our strength and encouragement in Him. His joy is not in any physical means by which men may reach a finish line, such as in the power of a horse or the legs of men. Rather God finds His joy in those sons who put their hope in Him and in the power of His unfailing love.

God's Word reminds us, "[We] are all sons of God through faith in Christ Jesus" (Galatians 3:26), and our God delights in His relationship with His sons just as every good father prides himself in the growth and accomplishments of his children. He invites us to communicate with Him regularly and often as we experience His Word and respond to His love in prayer.

As we press on toward our heavenly prize, God helps us to live our lives for Him. Many of God's faithful people, both men and women, have lived before us. Theirs is a heritage for us to build on and to pass on to those who will follow after us—our wives, children, friends, and others whose lives will be touched by the love and power of God demonstrated in our lives.

The writer to the Hebrews encourages us to live as men of faith, reminding us about where to keep our focus as we run life's race: "Therefore, since we are surrounded by such a great cloud of witnesses, let us throw off everything that hinders and the sin that so easily entangles, and let us run with perseverance the race marked out for us. Let us fix our eyes on Jesus, the author and perfecter of our faith, who for the joy set before Him endured the cross, scorning its shame, and sat down at the right hand of the throne of God. Consider Him who endured such opposition from sinful men, so that you will not grow weary and lose heart" (Hebrews 12:1–3).

God's blessings as you run the race and claim the prize already won for you!

About the Godly Man Series

The Godly Man series is especially for men. Written in book-study format, each course in the Godly Man series is organized into chapters suitable for either group or individual study. Periodically throughout each chapter, questions have been provided to further stimulate your thinking, assist you in personal application, and spark group discussion.

How to Use Each Course in the Godly Man Series

Each course in the Godly Man series has been prepared especially for small group settings. It may, however, be used as a self-study or in a traditional Sunday morning Bible class. Chapters of each course may be read in advance of group discussion. Or participants may take turns reading sections of the Bible study during your group study sessions.

Planning for a Small Group Study

1. *Select a leader* for the course or a leader for the day. It will be the leader's responsibility to secure needed materials, to keep the discussion moving, and to help involve all participants.

2. *Emphasize sharing.* Your class will work best if the participants feel comfortable with one another and if all feel their contributions to the class are important and useful. Take the necessary time at the beginning of the course to get to know one another. Share what you expect to gain from this course. Develop an atmosphere of openness, trust, and caring among the participants. Agree in advance that private issues shared during your study will remain within the group.

3. *Pray for one another.* Begin and conclude each study session with a prayer. Pray for one another, for your families, your work, and all other aspects of your life. Involve everyone. Consider praying-around-the-circle, with each person offering a specific prayer to God for the person on his left.

As You Plan to Lead the Group

1. Read this guide in its entirety before you lead the first session.

2. Use the Answers and Comments section in the back of the study.

3. Pray each day for those in your group.

4. Depend on the Holy Spirit. Expect His presence; He will guide you and cause you to grow. God will not let His Word return empty (Isaiah 55:11) as you study it individually or with others in a group.

5. Prepare well, studying each session's material thorough-

ly. Add your comments in the margins so that you may add your insights to spark conversation and discussion throughout the session.

6. Begin and end the session with prayer.

7. Begin and end on time. Punctuality is a courtesy to everyone and can be a factor to encourage discussion.

8. Find ways to keep the session informal; consider meeting over breakfast at a local restaurant or some other friendly setting where participants can be seated face to face.

9. Keep the class moving. Limit your discussion to questions of interest to the participants. Be selective. You don't need to cover every question. Note that most Bible references are included in the study guide. At times, however, you may want to look up and share additional insights provided by other suggested Bible references.

10. Build one another up through your fellowship and study. Make a conscious effort to support one another in your personal and professional challenges.

Expect and rejoice in God's presence and blessing as He builds your faith and enriches your life through the study of His Word.

Servant-Leadership:
An Introduction

1

Ready

Leadership is difficult to describe or define today because there appears to be no consensus about what constitutes effective leadership. As America transitions into a knowledge-based economy, many have questioned the effectiveness of traditional autocratic and hierarchical models of leadership. In the traditional autocratic model, the leader determines a plan of action and sees to it that the plan is carried out by subordinates. This traditional model has often worked quite well for us over the years and still works effectively in many organizations. However, some American businesses, schools, and government agencies have recently experimented with a new model of leadership characterized by cooperation, collaboration, and consensus-building. In the newer democratic model, the leader facilitates discussion among the workers of an organization, and together they determine a plan of action and monitor each other to see that the plan is carried out.

Common sense suggests that some leadership tasks lend themselves primarily to one model or the other. For example, if we're flying in a 747 and one of the engines flames out, we probably would want the pilot to act autocratically and decisively and to follow established procedures rather than to step into the cabin and facilitate a discussion among the passengers in order to reach a consensus before doing anything about the lost engine. On the other hand, if we work for the company that makes jet engines for the 747, we might welcome the chance to discuss with our leaders and coworkers the possible causes of engine failure, to collaborate on a plan of action to correct any design or production problems, and to agree to monitor each other to see that the plan is completed.

Complete the following brief exercise to help you consider and discuss these two very different leadership styles.

1. Describe a situation in which an autocratic leadership style seems to work best.

2. Describe a situation in which a democratic leadership style seems to work best.

3. In general, what type of leadership style do you prefer? Why?

4. Describe a situation in which you used an autocratic leadership style.

5. Describe a situation in which you used a democratic leadership style.

Whether the new democratic model of leadership represents a radical paradigm shift that is here to stay or a mere pendulum swing that will soon disappear remains to be seen, but changes in leadership style appear to be in the wind. This Bible study will reference both the old autocratic and newer democratic leadership styles but will primarily focus on a third tried-and-true model of leadership that some have called *servant-leadership*.

Robert K. Greenleaf first coined the term servant-leader in "The Servant as Leader," an essay he wrote in 1970 after he had retired from an executive position with AT&T. In his essay Greenleaf wrote the following about servant-leadership:

> It begins with the natural feeling that one wants to serve, to serve first. Then conscious choice brings one to aspire to lead. The difference manifests itself in the care taken by the servant—first to make sure that other people's highest-priority needs are being served. The best test is: Do those served grow as persons; do they, while being served,

become healthier, wiser, freer, more autonomous, more likely themselves to become servants?

(Greenleaf, Robert K. *Servant Leadership: A Journey into the Nature of Legitimate Power and Greatness.* [New York: Paulist Press, 1977], 13–14)

Even though Greenleaf coined the term several decades ago, the concept of servant-leadership can be traced back to biblical times—to the Old Testament patriarchs and prophets, to the perfect servant-leader, the Messiah Jesus Christ, and to the apostles of the New Testament.

Today's servant-leader may work in either a hierarchical or democratic organization but operates using the leadership model practiced and fulfilled by Jesus Christ two thousand years ago. Autocratic leaders and democratic leaders are largely task oriented; whether by command or by consensus, these leaders are most often intent on getting a job accomplished. Servant-leaders, on the other hand, are always people oriented. They are concerned with the spiritual, emotional, and physical well-being of people. Servant-leaders can work effectively in autocratic or democratic organizations to create a vision or to achieve goals, but those goals and visions always focus on service to people, not simply on making money, getting a job done, or sustaining an organization. It is probably easier to practice servant-leadership within a democratic organization because the organization is structured to be concerned about the opinions of its workers. However, an organization can be democratic in name only. Its leaders may in fact have their eyes only on the bottom line or on their own advancement within the organization. On the other hand, servant-leadership can be found in some autocratic organizations. There is probably no better example of an autocratic organization in America than the military, but the best officers, whose primary concern is the well-being of the personnel entrusted to their care, may also be considered servant-leaders.

Read

Read Jesus' response to a mother's request that her sons, James and John, be placed in high positions of leadership:

Then the mother of Zebedee's sons came to Jesus with her sons and, kneeling down, asked a favor of Him.

"What is it you want?" He asked.

She said, "Grant that one of these two sons of mine

may sit at Your right and the other at Your left in Your kingdom."

"You don't know what you are asking," Jesus said to them. "Can you drink the cup I am going to drink?"

"We can," they answered.

Jesus said to them, "You will indeed drink from My cup, but to sit at My right or left is not for Me to grant. These places belong to those for whom they have been prepared by My Father."

When the ten heard about this, they were indignant with the two brothers. Jesus called them together and said, "You know that the rulers of the Gentiles lord it over them, and their high officials exercise authority over them. Not so with you. Instead, whoever wants to be first among you must be your servant, and whoever wants to be first must be your slave—just as the Son of Man did not come to be served, but to serve, and to give His life as a ransom for many." (Matthew 20:20–28)

React

1. What erroneous assumption did James and John and their mother (and for that matter the other disciples) make about Jesus' leadership?

2. What did Jesus mean when He asked James and John, "Can you drink the cup I am going to drink?" For help read Matthew 26:36–46 and Isaiah 55:22.

3. What did Jesus mean when He told all His disciples, "Whoever wants to become great among you must be your servant"?

Read

The servant-leadership of Jesus was foretold by the prophet Isaiah about seven hundred years before Jesus' birth. Read the prophet's words from Isaiah 52:13–53:12.

See, My servant will act wisely;
He will be raised and lifted up and highly exalted.
Just as there were many who were appalled at Him—
His appearance was so disfigured beyond that of any
man
and His form marred beyond human likeness—
so will He sprinkle many nations,
and kings will shut their mouths because of Him.
For what they were not told, they will see,
and what they have not heard, they will understand.
Who has believed our message
and to whom has the arm of the LORD been revealed?
He grew up before Him like a tender shoot,
and like a root out of dry ground.
He had no beauty or majesty to attract us to Him,
nothing in His appearance that we should desire Him.
He was despised and rejected by men,
a man of sorrows, and familiar with suffering.
Like one from whom men hide their faces
He was despised, and we esteemed Him not.
Surely He took up our infirmities
and carried our sorrows,
yet we considered Him stricken by God,
smitten by Him, and afflicted.
But He was pierced for our transgressions,
He was crushed for our iniquities;
the punishment that brought us peace was upon Him,
and by His wounds we are healed.
We all, like sheep, have gone astray,
each of us has turned to His own way;
and the LORD has laid on Him
the iniquity of us all.
He was oppressed and afflicted,
yet He did not open His mouth;
He was led like a lamb to the slaughter,
and as a sheep before her shearers is silent,
so He did not open His mouth.
By oppression and judgment He was taken away.
And who can speak of His descendants?
For He was cut off from the land of the living;
for the transgression of my people He was stricken.
He was assigned a grave with the wicked,

and with the rich in His death,
though He had done no violence,
nor was any deceit in His mouth.
Yet it was the LORD's will to crush Him and cause Him to
suffer,
and though the LORD makes His life a guilt offering,
He will see His offspring and prolong His days,
and the will of the LORD will prosper in His hand.
After the suffering of His soul,
He will see the light of life and be satisfied;
by His knowledge My righteous servant will justify many,
and He will bear their iniquities.
Therefore I will give Him a portion among the great,
and He will divide the spoils with the strong,
because He poured out His life unto death,
and was numbered with the transgressors.
For He bore the sin of many,
and made intercession for the transgressors.

REACT

1. One of the paradoxes of servant-leadership in the con-
text of the Christian life is that servant-leaders often suffer
even as they accomplish great things as they serve others. Note
how this section from Isaiah is organized. The reading begins
with an acknowledgment of the servant's ultimate triumph,
continues with a lengthy description of the servant's suffering,
and ends with the Lord's promise to reward the faithful servant. Circle the specific passages that reveal the loneliness and
pain of the servant-leader; underline those passages that show
the triumph and joy of the servant-leader.

2. What are some of the possible risks we face when we
practice servant-leadership? What are some of the joys we can
anticipate as we practice servant-leadership?

Read

The evening before Jesus suffered and died, He modeled servant-leadership for His disciples during their Passover Feast. Read the story from John 13 as retold by Walter Wangerin Jr.

At evening Jesus entered the upper room with ten of the disciples. Simon and John met them there. The table was neatly set. Already the prescribed foods had been brought in, filling the room with a rich aroma: lamb, unleavened bread, a sauce of bitter herbs, wine.

The table, low to the ground, was shaped like a C so the servants could enter the middle and approach each place. One would not sit at such a formal meal. The table was furnished with low couches on three sides of it; one reclined on these.

The room was spare. There were few ornaments in the house of the Essenes. Along the wall another narrower table held water and towels. A rug received the sandals of the people as they came in. Already the candles were lit. It was dusk outside. Breezes bent the candle flames. Shadows were gathering at the high ceiling.

Jesus, when he had removed his sandals, went to a central place at the table. The others found places to the left and the right of him. Jesus motioned them to recline. So, in a genial ripple of motion and chatter, the twelve disciples lay down on the couches, crooked their left elbows, and propped their heads on their hands.

Jesus continued to stand, looking down both sides of the table.

"I—" he said, "With all my heart I have earnestly desired to eat this Passover among you before I suffer—"

Conversation ceased. Faces tilted toward him: his people, frowning, questioning, exhibiting surprise and a sudden blinking pity—his foolish people, still ignorant of what was to be, though he had told them; he had told them! He had said it clearly and often. His poor sheep-people, his munching followers, his disciples.

"I tell you, I will not eat it again until it is fulfilled in the kingdom of God."

While they watched him, then, Jesus shed his robe and went to the side table and picked up a clean towel and tied it around his waist in the manner of a servant. He gathered his hair in another towel, which he wound as a turban around his head. He poured water into a pitcher and carried it to the nearest disciple, and the last one in sequence around the table. Then, in a room completely hushed, Jesus knelt down and began to wash that disciple's feet.

He moved to the next and washed his feet, too.

And the next.

So still was the room, that each small splash of water could be heard.

Andrew began silently to cry.

So did Judas, though his eyes were wide open and blazing with an odd ferocity. Jesus felt that Judas' feet twitched the instant he touched them, and he knew: cosmic elements, light and darkness, were contending in the poor disciple's soul.

He moved on, then, to Philip and Matthew and James and the blunt, frowning Thomas.

Last of all, Jesus came to Simon.

Simon Peter, forever proud of his humilities!—he snatched his thick feet back beneath his robe and said, "What! Are you going to wash my feet?"

Jesus sighed and said, "You may not now understand what I'm doing, but you will in the future."

"No!" Simon said, his bare jowls trembling. "You will never wash my feet."

Something tightened in Jesus' throat. "If I do not wash you," he said, striving for kindness in his voice, "if you do not let me serve you, you will have no part in me."

Simon shot his feet out again, pleading, "My hands, too, Lord! Wash my hands and my head!"

As he rubbed the hard soles of Simon Peter's feet, and then again as he toweled them dry, Jesus said, "Those who have bathed do not need to wash—except for their feet—for they are clean all over."

By now the light outside the lattices had diminished to a deep blue. The room trembled and shifted in yellow candle flame.

Jesus removed the towels and laid them again on the side table. He put his arms through the short sleeves of his own robe, shook his hair free, and took his place, reclining among the disciples.

"Do you understand what I've just done to you?" he said. "You call me Teacher and Lord, and you are right because that's what I am. Now: if I, your Lord and Teacher, have washed your feet, then you, too, must wash one another's feet. This is an example. Blessed are you, my friends, if you do it!"

(Wangerin, Walter Jr. *The Book of God*. [Grand Rapids, Michigan: Zondervan, 1996], 778–80)

REACT

1. What presuppositions about leadership did the disciples possess that kept them from understanding why Jesus would want to wash their feet?

2. What lesson does Jesus attempt to teach the disciples in His washing of their feet?

3. Why would most of us be moved or shocked or embarrassed to have a similar act of service performed for us today by someone of great authority or position? (For example: Why might it move, shock, or embarrass you if the governor of your state came to your house to wash your car?)

4. What was Jesus' greatest act of servant-leadership performed not only for the disciples who shared the Passover with Him in the upper room, but also for all other disciples then, now, and in the future? How does this act demonstrate servant-leadership to you? See Luke 23:26–46.

READ

As time permits, look up the following Bible passages and note how the apostolic leaders of the early church identified themselves as servants of Jesus Christ:

Romans 1:1

Galatians 1:10

Philippians 1:1

2 Timothy 2:24

Titus 1:1

James 1:1

2 Peter 1:1

Jude 1

Revelation 1:1

Respond

In this chapter we have briefly considered two models of leadership—the autocratic and the democratic—and we have learned a little bit about servant-leadership as exemplified by the words and actions of Jesus Christ, the Messiah. We have also noted that servant-leadership is probably easier to practice in a democratic work environment but that some autocratic leaders, who primarily focus on their workers, can be considered servant-leaders.

Is it possible to become a perfect servant-leader who is always motivated to serve his employee or coworkers? Absolutely not. Such perfection is not possible in flawed human beings. It is possible, though, by God's grace, to become more Christ-like in our roles as leaders. With this goal, we pray for the Holy Spirit's strength and guidance as we study the characteristics of servant-leaders in our next five lessons.

For now, however:

1. Write something specific you can do this week that will enable you to demonstrate servant-leadership. (Remember that a servant-leader is primarily concerned about serving people and enabling them to become servant-leaders themselves!)

2. Pray that the Lord will guide your efforts and forgive your shortcomings as you attempt to demonstrate servant-leadership in your church, your home, your school, and your place of employment.

COMMITMENT AND THE SERVANT-LEADER

Ready

Commitment is one of the characteristics or qualities of a servant-leader. A leader's commitment to God-pleasing tasks and to the people working to accomplish those tasks is essential to a leader's ability to lead effectively. Total commitment on the part of the leader to a project can engender an enthusiasm so contagious that people will often volunteer to help the leader accomplish the task. Enthusiastic, committed leaders attract talented people to a worthwhile project. Add a leader's commitment to the growth of people involved in the project, and people will be empowered to carry on the task even if the leader steps aside or moves on to empower other people to accomplish another project.

In this chapter we will examine how commitment to a cause and commitment to people characterize a servant-leader. We will end with a discussion of biblical servant-leaders who exhibited a commitment to their followers. But we'll begin this chapter with a look at two athletic coaches who were successful in a profession usually noted for its autocratic leadership style. Both coaches, however, enjoyed great success while exhibiting servant-leadership characteristics in dealing with their players and assistant coaches.

Before you read on, though, think about one of your favorite or least favorite coaches, and describe what made him or her a good or bad coach. (If you want, define "coach" broadly enough to include band, choir, and theater directors, Scout masters, drill sergeants, etc.)

Read

John Wooden was arguably the best coach in the history of college basketball. During his years as UCLA's coach, Wooden was certainly a servant-leader who exemplified an unusually strong commitment to the game of basketball and to his players. The legendary Wooden, who played on the 1927 Indiana

State High School championship team and on two national championship teams at Purdue in 1930 and 1932, coached for 27 years at UCLA and is the only man ever elected to college basketball's hall of fame as both a player and a coach. During his tenure as head coach, the Bruins had an .813 winning percentage, produced a record 10 NCAA titles, and at one time won 88 games in a row. No college basketball coach has come even close to matching Wooden's record.

To what can John Wooden's success in large part be attributed? To his commitment to his players. This commitment is exemplified in an incident related in the first chapter of his book *They Call Me Coach*. In the opening pages of this chapter, Wooden talks about his concern for John Slaughter, a player who was disappointed in not playing very long in a championship game:

> As I turned away from the post-game press conference and headed down that long corridor in Kansas City toward the dressing room, my feet and spirits dragged. For while I looked forward to congratulating the team on their victory, my thoughts were also on Fred Slaughter. What was he feeling at this moment?
>
> Throughout the entire season, Fred had started every game. He had a brilliant year. Fred was a totally unselfish player with great team devotion and was frequently asked to do things for which a player receives little public attention. Even though he was short for a college center, barely 6 feet 5 inches tall, Fred was the blocker, screener, and rebounder—things seldom seen and appreciated by the crowd. But in his final game for the championship with Duke he had gotten off to a bad start. As the game moved along, it got worse instead of better. Finally, a change had to be made, so I pulled Fred and put in Doug McIntosh. And Doug did such a fine job that I left him in until the game was ours.
>
> While I walked along toward the dressing room, George Moriarty's words were ringing in my mind, "Who can ask more of a man than giving all within his span? Giving all, it seems to me, is not so far from victory." And yet I knew that Fred was not alone in his disappointment. Having grown up not too far away in Topeka, Kansas, where he had attended high school, he was well aware that the crowd had been pretty well sprinkled with Slaughter relatives and fans.
>
> Pushing the dressing room door, I ran right into Fred. He had evidently been waiting for me. "Coach," he said, "before someone gets the wrong impression, I want you to know that I understand. You had to leave Doug in there because he played so well, and I didn't. I wanted to play in the worst way, but I do understand, and if anyone says I was upset, it's not true. Disappointed, yes, but upset, no. And I was very happy for Doug."
>
> You know, there are a lot of peaks and valleys in every coach's life. But

this was the peak—the ultimate. We had just won our first, and my first, NCAA title by whipping Duke 98 to 83 and closed out the 1964 season with a perfect 30 and 0 record. But my concern for Fred had damaged all of that until this moment.

(Wooden, John. *They Call Me Coach.* [Waco, Texas: Word Books, 1972], 9–10)

Imagine that! John Wooden identifies as the peak experience of his first NCAA championship his conversation with a disappointed, understanding player after the game. Wooden's greatness as a basketball coach can certainly be traced to a number of attributes including knowledge of the sport, the ability to teach the fundamentals of the game and to organize effective practices, enthusiasm, a fierce desire to win, and a strong work ethic, but he begins his book with an anecdote about his commitment to a player's well-being. That's both incredible and altogether refreshing when read in light of what has happened to much of college athletics in the last 35 years!

REACT

In a more recent book, Wooden reiterates the importance of a coach's commitment to players in a section called "Dictator Leaders":

There are coaches out there who have won championships with a dictator approach, among them Vince Lombardi and Bobby Knight. I had a different philosophy. I didn't want to be a dictator to my players or assistant coaches or managers. For me, concern, compassion, and consideration were always priorities of the highest order.

(Wooden, John. *Wooden: A Lifetime of Observations and Reflections On and Off the Court.* [Lincolnwood, Illinois: Contemporary Books, 1997], 117)

1. Defend or refute: John Wooden's approach to his players and to his task may have worked for him, but the approach would not work in most other environments.

2. Defend or refute the following: Some players respect dictatorial coaches, and some workers respect dictatorial leaders because dictatorial methods often get results.

Read

It appears that John Wooden's commitment to his players was centered in his spiritual beliefs. Read what he has to say about the Christian life:

> In my profession, I must be deeply concerned with God's belief in me and be truly interested in the welfare of my fellow-man. No coach should be trusted with the tremendous responsibility of handling young men under the great mental, emotional, and physical strain to which they are subjected unless he is spiritually strong. If he does possess this inner strength, it is only because he has faith and truly loves his fellow-man. ... The coach who is committed to the Christlike life will be helping youngsters under his supervision to develop wholesome disciplines of body, mind, and spirit that will build character worthy of his Master's calling. He must set the proper example by word and by deed. It is not easy.

(Wooden, *They Call Me Coach,* 94)

React

1. Defend or refute: A coach's first priority should be the physical, mental, and spiritual development of his players.

2. Defend or refute: A leader should center attention on workers first and on tasks second.

Read

Tom Osborne was one of the best coaches in the modern era of college football. As coach of the Nebraska Cornhuskers for 25 seasons, Osborne's teams won three national championships (1994, 1995, and 1997) and compiled a record of 255-49-3 for a winning percentage of .839. Still an active member of the Fellowship of Christian Athletes, Osborne has been the recipient of many awards including the American Football Coach of the Year Award and the Father Flanagan Award for

Service to Youth. Before he retired, Osborne and his wife, Nancy, initiated the Husker Teammates program that matched Nebraska football players with junior high school students in big-brother relationships. Known for his professional demeanor on and off the playing field and his willingness to work hard for the betterment of his players, his coaches, and his program, Osborne came to represent the best of college football leadership during his 25 years as Nebraska's head coach.

Probably the lowest point in Osborne's career, but also the point where Osborne's commitment to his players was most evident, occurred during the 1995 football season. The season eventually culminated in a national championship, but, as Osborne tells it in his book *On Solid Ground,* it was a year filled with adversity, a year filled with serious allegations made against several talented Nebraska players. As a prelude to telling how he dealt with those serious allegations, Osborne talks about his own Christian faith and how his faith influenced the way he treated his players:

> Sometimes people say, "It doesn't matter what you believe since all religions are really the same." As I have studied the religions of the world, it seems that nearly all, except Christianity, ignore the idea of grace. And grace is what I am greatly in need of. I have come to the understanding that I fall so far short of godly perfection that it's only by grace that I can possibly be approved in God's eyes.
>
> As I have gotten older, the concept of grace has affected me more and more. As a younger man, I unwisely tended to think that I could achieve a great many things through my own efforts—even God's approval. The longer I've lived, the more I realize that I have been able to earn very little that has lasting value through my own efforts.
>
> Tom Landry, the former coach of the Dallas Cowboys, apparently arrived in his belief system at the same place I have. In his autobiography Tom stated: "The most important lesson I've learned in my life is that God is so gracious that He accepts me, my failures, my personality quirks, my shortcomings and all. It's hard for a perfectionist like me, but I have to admit I can never be good enough. No matter how sound my strategy, how much I study, how hard I work—I'll always be a failure when it comes to being perfect. Yet God loves me anyway."
>
> ... I've watched many players over the years commit their lives to God. Each time a player has turned away from his own devices and put his life in God's hands, I've wit-

nessed a change in attitude and behavior. It's only by God's grace that any of us can truly love ourselves and others.

As I think about the dilemma many young people find themselves in today, I believe it is only through God's love and grace that many of them will experience forgiveness and meaning in life.

... I realize many don't share this belief with me. But it's important for me to write about my faith because it affects the way I act. Having experienced grace in my life, I hope to be a little less judgmental, a little more forgiving, and a whole lot more appreciative of the fact that someone like me could be considered worthy of God's love.

I hope that my conduct honors God as I deal with players, coaches, my family, and with how I use the resources that I have been given. I realize I fall far short of honoring Him at times, but I also realize this is why I need God's grace.

(Osborne, Tom. *On Solid Ground.* [Lincoln, Nebraska: Nebraska Book Company, 1996], 125–28)

Because Coach Osborne was keenly aware of God's unmerited love and grace toward him demonstrated in the person and work of Jesus, he was able to love and forgive his wayward players in return even though many sportswriters (outside of Nebraska!) criticized him for being too forgiving and accused Osborne of sacrificing his principles for the sake of winning football games. But toward the end of *On Solid Ground,* Osborne makes it clear that rather than sacrificing his principles, he was actually practicing them. In his book he details the accusations against some of his players and his decision to discipline and forgive them, and then explains why he offered a second chance to the players who had been accused of misconduct.

REACT

1. Recall a time in your life when you were the recipient of well-deserved discipline.

2. Recall a time in your life when you were the recipient of unmerited grace.

3. Suggest a one-sentence guideline for the use of discipline and correction on the part of a servant-leader who is committed to the growth of his workers.

4. Suggest a one-sentence guideline for the use of unmerited forgiveness on the part of a servant-leader who is committed to the growth of his workers.

Read

When he was 25 years old, Hezekiah succeeded his father, Ahaz, as king of Judah. Hezekiah's challenge was to right the wrongs of his father's reign, for his father had ignored the commands of God in an effort to appease his enemies. During his reign Ahaz had removed the furnishings from the temple in Jerusalem, closed the temple doors, and promoted the worship of Baal and Moloch by erecting altars to pagan gods on every street corner in Jerusalem. Before you read about the servant-leadership of Hezekiah, read about his father Ahaz's failure to commit himself to God's will and to his people's welfare in 2 Chronicles 28:1–4 and 16–26.

React

One of the most telling statements about Ahaz is found in verse 22: "In his time of trouble King Ahaz became even more unfaithful to the LORD." This, of course, is the antithesis of the commitment exhibited by a true servant-leader. Why did Ahaz cave in to the paganism practiced by his enemies? Can you think of any contemporary leaders who, in times of financial or political troubles, have deserted their principles to the detriment of their followers?

Read

In preparation for reading about Hezekiah from 2 Chronicles 29, read Walter Wangerin Jr.'s paraphrase of the story:

For the rest of that day King Hezekiah sat in a dark corner of the temple, contemplating what the prophet [Isaiah] had said. It required a whole new view of the God of Israel. But, oh!—what a glorious sight was spread before him now! As if he stood on a mountain, and the world lay down before him.

The Lord was not lesser, but greater than the king had conceived! And if a people perished, it was not because God had forgotten them, but because they had forgotten God.

"He is our strength," Hezekiah murmured, weaving the meaning of his name into the word.

And how did Israel forget the Lord? Their rituals were more elaborate than Judah could afford. Their ceremonies were rich and noisy, splendid displays. But they did not remember the covenant. They had lost humility and obedience. Doing good.

"God is my refuge and strength," the king said. His voice echoed in the empty temple. A little daylight drifted through dust in the upper reaches of the room—a cruel light, really, because the sacred place was cluttered with junk, wooden images, the sins of the fathers. Idols. Abominations.

The king stood up and spoke in a full voice:

"God is our refuge and strength! Therefore we will not fear though the nations change, though the mountains shake in the heart of the sea, though the waters roar and foam!"

He walked to the lampstands that Solomon had fashioned two hundred years ago. They were gathered all along one side, dead out.

"This," he said, "should be the habitation of the Most High God"—then he walked out into sunlight and stood on the porch of Solomon's temple. He saw a priest in the courtyard and called him over.

"God," said the long, lugubrious king, "is in the midst of us. We shall not be moved."

"No, sir," said the priest. "We shall not be moved."

The king frowned, deepening the lines between his brows. He pondered the priest a moment, then he said, "Do you believe that?"

"I believe that the Lord of hosts is with us. Yes, my lord: I believe it."

The king said, "And I'll tell you another thing: it is the Lord who causes desolations in the earth! Likewise, the Lord can stop war altogether."

"He shatters the spear and burns the chariots with fire."

"Extraordinary!" the king murmured, gazing grey-eyed at the man before him. "Priest, what is your name?"

The priest said, "Azariah."

The king said, "Azariah, work with me. I appoint you the chief officer of the house of God. Gather the priests and Levites. Command them to sanctify themselves. It is now time to purge the temple and again to sanctify it!"

In those days a great reform took place in Jerusalem and in all Judah.

All the desecrations that had accumulated in the temple were carried outside the city and thrown into the brook Kidron, where they were burned. The temple doors were repaired and opened. The altars were purified, the utensils, the lampstands, and the room which in darkness contained the Ark of the Covenant, the Holy of Holies.

Hezekiah then led Judah in a sacrifice of thanksgiving.

(Wangerin, *The Book of God*, 445–46)

Read

Now read the account of Hezekiah's commitment to God's commands as written in 2 Chronicles 29:1–36.

React

1. For those who aspire to become committed servant-leaders, what lesson about responding to evil is taught in the opening words of verse 3, "In the first month of the first year of his reign ... " and in the closing words of verse 36, " ... because it was done so quickly"? Confirm this lesson by citing an anecdote from your own experience.

2. Why did the priests and Levites follow the leadership of Hezekiah in purifying the temple in Jerusalem?

3. How is Hezekiah's commitment to the task exemplified in verse 29: "When the offerings were finished, the king and everyone present with him knelt down and worshiped"? What implications for servant-leadership are suggested in this verse?

Read

The story of Stephen, the church's first martyr, begins with a commitment to servant-leadership. Some background to Stephen's story: for the first year or so after Pentecost, it appears that the apostles administered all of the affairs—both spiritual and practical—of the church in Jerusalem, but, when a dispute arose between Grecian Jewish believers and Hebraic Jewish believers over the daily distribution of food to their widows, the apostles decided to choose seven men to serve food to all of the widows. Stephen, "a man full of God's grace and power," was one of the seven chosen to wait on tables! Read about Stephen's commitment to his faith in Christ in both word and deed. Begin by reading Acts, chapter 6.

React

1. Stephen the table waiter apparently was also a skilled, Spirit-filled debater. Why do you think such a talented individual was willing to perform the mundane task of serving the widows their daily allotment of food?

2. In the service of speaking God's truth, Stephen was seized and falsely accused. Recall a time when for the sake of your faith, you were mistreated, misunderstood, made fun of, or shunned.

Read

You may want to skim Acts 7:1–53, which records Stephen's speech to the Sanhedrin. In this speech Stephen first summarizes the history of the Old Testament, and then he concludes by condemning his listeners for their role in the crucifixion of Jesus. After you skim this speech, read about the stoning of Stephen in Acts 7:54–60.

REACT

Servant-leadership can be dangerous. So committed was Stephen to leading the Jewish people in Jerusalem to the truth about Jesus Christ that he was stoned to death for speaking the very words that could have turned his murderers' lives toward heaven.

1. Note that verse 60 shows how faithful Stephen was to his message, to the people whom he hoped to reach, and to his role as servant until the very end of his life. What enabled Stephen to demonstrate his persistence and commitment?

2. Note also that the words of Jesus at His death recorded in Luke 23:34, "Father, forgive them, for they do not know what they are doing," parallel Stephen's dying words. In terms of servant-leadership, what connections can be made between the life and death of Stephen and the life and death of Jesus?

Respond

Take a few minutes to consider how you can more effectively demonstrate your commitment to the leadership tasks God has provided to you—whether those tasks are centered in your family, your job, your community, or your church. Then explain how you can practice true servant-leadership through your commitment to the growth of your coworkers or those over whom you have authority. In other words, explain how you can become a better servant-leader by recommitting yourself to your tasks and to the betterment of those with whom you work. How might the commitment you demonstrate provide you the opportunity to share with others that Jesus willingly suffered and died for your sins and through His death you have received the gift of eternal life?

3 **WINSOMENESS** AND THE **SERVANT-LEADER**

Ready

An effective servant-leader has the ability to win some winsomely to his cause. In other words, a servant-leader persuades workers that a cause or project is worth doing and provides encouragement along the way. Winsome persuasion calls for tact on the part of the leader, but more importantly it calls for a genuine respect for the diverse talents of all workers and a willingness to encourage and affirm workers as they do their tasks. A winsome servant-leader must step aside once workers have been empowered to carry on the task and be willing to let others receive whatever accolades might be given at the completion of a task.

Recall the last time you willingly and joyfully participated in a worthwhile project or task, and describe the role the leader(s) of that project played in persuading you to participate and in making it a gratifying activity.

Read

One of Aesop's fables speaks to the issue of winsomeness. Written perhaps six centuries before Christ, "The Wind and the Sun" tells of a competition won through the power of persuasion:

> A dispute once arose between the Wind and the Sun, which was the stronger of the two, and they agreed to put the point upon this issue, that whichever soonest made a traveler take off his cloak, should be accounted the more powerful. The Wind began, and blew with all his might and main a blast, cold and fierce as a Thracian storm; but the stronger he blew, the closer the traveler wrapped his cloak around him, and the tighter he grasped it with his hands. Then broke out the Sun: with his welcome beams he dispersed the vapor and the cold; the traveler felt the genial warmth, and as the Sun shone brighter and brighter, he sat down, overcome with the heat, and cast his cloak on the ground.
>
> Thus the Sun was declared the conqueror; and it has

ever been deemed that persuasion is better than force; and
that the sunshine of a kind and gentle manner will sooner
lay open a poor man's heart than all the threatenings and
force of blustering authority.

(James, Thomas. *Aesop's Fables: A New Version, Chiefly from the Original
Sources.* [London: Richard Clay, 1898])

REACT

1. Describe a time when you were forced to do something
you did not want to do by someone in authority. What was your
attitude toward the forceful authority figure?

2. Resentment against authority is often the reaction when
we are forced to do something against our will. However, you
may find that years later some people express gratitude toward
an authority figure who made them do something that they at
first resented. Often, though, those forceful authority figures
exhibited at other times qualities of kindness and concern or
honesty and integrity that endeared them to those who were
subject to their authoritative commands. Can you recall a situation when initial resentment gradually turned into gratitude
toward a forceful authority figure?

3. Now describe a time when you were persuaded to do
something you did not want to do by someone in authority.
What was your attitude toward the persuasive authority figure?

4. Based on your own experiences and on those of your
group members, evaluate the moral of "The Wind and the Sun."
Is the moral—"that persuasion is better than force"—always
true? Never true? Often true? Why?

Read

In his *Autobiography*, Ben Franklin writes that as a leader he often expressed himself in "terms of modest diffidence" to win others to his point of view. What he is talking about here is winsome persuasion. Franklin says that whenever he suggested any proposal that might be met with opposition, he refrained from using the words "certainly, undoubtedly," or any other words "that gave the air of positiveness to an opinion." Rather Franklin often used the words "I conceive, or I apprehend a thing to be so or so, it appears to me, or I should think it is so or so for such and such reasons, or I imagine it to be so, or it is so if I am not mistaken." Franklin says, "This habit I believe has been of great advantage to me, when I have had occasion to inculcate my opinions and persuade men into measures that I have been from time to time engaged in promoting."

React

1. How a leader phrases a statement can have a great impact on those whom the leader wishes to influence. Evaluate the potential effectiveness of the following pairs of statements on those hearing them:

A. No one is going to tell me that we should not leave tomorrow morning at 5:00 A.M. sharp for the Habitat for Humanity site. Be there on time or get left behind.
B. It appears to me that we'll have to leave by 5:00 A.M. tomorrow morning for the Habitat for Humanity site. If we don't, we might be late. What do you think?

A. If I'm not mistaken, the Christmas tree would look better if it were moved a few more feet away from the pulpit. Let's try moving it and see how it looks.
B. Move the blessed Christmas tree away from the pulpit, you tinselheads. Can't you do anything right?

A. I think we made a wrong turn back there.
B. You made a wrong turn back there.

A. Fire! Get out of the building! Now!!

B. It appears to me that we should vacate the premises in short order lest we singe our flesh. What do you think?

2. Ben Franklin was one of the most intelligent, creative individuals of his time, yet he was careful to phrase his statements in such a way that they persuaded rather than offended. Among your acquaintances, who are the best practitioners of "modest diffidence"? What are some of the phrases that they use to create a sense of servant-leadership?

Read

In his book *Lincoln on Leadership,* Donald T. Phillips argues that Abraham Lincoln was a skilled practitioner of persuasion. In a chapter titled "Persuade Rather Than Coerce," Phillips describes Lincoln as decisive without being offensive and cites the following passage from one of Lincoln's speeches that clearly enunciates Lincoln's attitude toward persuasion:

> When the conduct of men is designed to be influenced, persuasion, kind, unassuming persuasion, should ever be adopted. It is an old and a true maxim, that a "drop of honey catches more flies than a gallon of gall." So with men. If you would win a man to your cause, first convince him that you are his sincere friend. Therein is a drop of honey that catches his heart, which, say what he will, is the great high road to his reason, and which, when once gained, you will find but little trouble in convincing his judgment of the justice of your cause, if indeed that cause really be a just one. On the contrary, assume to dictate to his judgment, or to command his action, or to mark him as one to be shunned and despised, and he will retreat within himself, close all the avenues to his head and his heart; and tho' your cause be naked truth itself ... you shall no more be able to [reach] him, than to penetrate the hard shell of a tortoise with a rye straw.
>
> Such is man, and so must he be understood by those who would lead him, even to his own best interest.

(Quoted in Phillips, Donald T. *Lincoln on Leadership.* [New York: Warner Books, 1992], 39–40)

REACT

Lincoln asserts that relationship building is a necessary prelude to successful persuasion and that people are persuaded to action more through appeals to their heart than through appeals to their head if the cause is just and good. In other words, friendship is better than logic when it comes to persuading someone to do something.

1. Why are we more likely to be persuaded to action by the clumsy, inarticulate encouragement of a friend than by the clear, irrefutable logic of a stranger?

2. Describe how a servant-leader you know well built a relationship with you that engendered trust and a willingness to follow his lead or participate in a cause he championed.

Read

Human beings are readily persuaded to do something they consider meaningful, but they often resist even the most winsome attempts to persuade them to do something they consider inconsequential. To complicate the issue, human beings differ widely in their assumptions of what is meaningful and what is not. Some find meaning in creative activity; others would rather follow step-by-step instructions. Some find meaning in relationships with people; others would rather read about people's relationships. Some find meaning in strenuous physical activity; others would rather sit and watch the sun set.

The perceptive servant-leader recognizes that meaningful activity is often defined differently by individuals, and, even when an overall goal is considered meaningful by all those working toward the goal, not all the individual tasks that get the group to the goal may be considered meaningful or necessary to all the participants. If a church group has decided to put on a summer musical in the school gymnasium, it's goal is clear: produce a show. However, do the carpenters who build the set necessarily care that the printed program is free of spelling errors? Does the copy editor of the program necessarily care that the makeup of the fourth girl in the back of the chorus is applied evenly? Do the people in charge of makeup necessarily care that the refreshment stand is properly stocked by intermission of each production?

Even though what individuals in a group find meaningful or important varies from person to person, it is generally true that people tend to find true meaning—not just transitory pleasure—in activities that are done for the benefit of others. When the carpenter, the editor, the makeup artist, and the Pepsi provider can be persuaded that they are working to serve an audience or working for the benefit of each other, they will work with an uncommon sense of purpose and commitment. Consider these words of Viktor Frankl, a survivor of the Holocaust and a psychiatrist who helped people develop a sense of meaning in their lives:

> The true meaning of life is to be discovered in the world rather than within man or his own psyche, as though it were a closed system. I have termed this constitutive characteristic "the self-transcendence of human existence." It denotes the fact that being human always points, and is directed, to something, or someone, other than oneself—be it a meaning to fulfill or another human being to encounter. The more one forgets himself—by giving himself to a cause to serve or another person to love— the more human he is and the more he actualizes himself. What is called self-actualization is not an attainable aim at all, for the simple reason that the more one would strive for it, the more he would miss it. In other words, self-actualization is possible only as a side-effect of self-transcendence.

(Frankl, Viktor. *Man's Search for Meaning*. [New York: Washington Square Press, 1959], 133)

An explanation of Frankl's last sentence might go something like this: Self-fulfillment cannot be attained when a person is focused on his own happiness, but self-fulfillment is possible only when one looks beyond one's self-centeredness and begins to serve others. This paradoxical truth is not, of course, news to a Christian, for it is the essence of the Christian life and is stated by Jesus in Matthew 10:39: "Whoever finds his life will lose it, and whoever loses his life for My sake will find it."

The servant-leader, then, may have his greatest success when he helps people discover that true meaning is to be found not in self-centeredness, but in genuine service to others. This servant attitude and action flows from the servant attitude and action Jesus demonstrated when He gave up His own security and safety to suffer and to die on the cross.

REACT

1. In what or in whom do you find meaning? Why?

2. Describe a time when you felt unfulfilled after you engaged in a predominantly self-serving activity.

3. Describe a time when you found fulfillment (somewhat unexpectedly, perhaps) in serving someone else.

4. What do you think Jesus meant when He told His followers, "Whoever loses his life for My sake will find it"? What might Jesus' words mean to us today? How did Jesus act on His words for our sake?

READ

For a servant-leader to persuade winsomely and sincerely, the leader must truly love and respect those he attempts to lead. Any phoniness or hypocrisy on the part of the leader will readily be detected (especially among young people!) and will ultimately lead to failure. The best guard against hypocrisy is the development of a sincere love of and respect for those you lead and serve. To develop respect for all individuals in a group is made easier if the gifts and talents of all are recognized by the servant-leader. To help you gain an appreciation for the diverse talents of individuals, read the following list of different types of intelligence identified by Dr. Howard Gardner and Thomas Hatch in their article entitled "Multiple Intelligences Go to School":

A. *Logical Mathematical* includes sensitivity to, and capacity to discern, logical or numerical patterns; ability to handle long chains of reasoning.

B. *Linguistic* relates to sensitivity to the sounds, rhythms, and meanings of words; sensitivity to the different functions of language.

C. *Musical* includes the ability to produce and appreciate rhythm, pitch, and timbre; appreciation of the forms of musical expressiveness.

D. *Spatial* includes capacities to perceive a visual-spatial world accurately and to perform transformations on one's initial perceptions.

E. *Bodily kinesthetic* is related to the abilities to control one's body movements and to handle objects skillfully.

F. *Interpersonal* includes the capacities to discern and respond appropriately to the moods, temperaments, motivations, and desires of other people.

G. *Intrapersonal* is based on the ability to access one's own feelings and the ability to discriminate among them and draw upon them to guide behavior; knowledge of one's own strengths, weaknesses, desires, and intelligences.

(Gardner, Howard, and Thomas Hatch. "Multiple Intelligences Go to School." *Educational Researcher* 18, no. 8 [November 1989], 6)

REACT

Although Gardner's theory of multiple intelligences is somewhat controversial, his identification of seven different aptitudes may help us recognize the gifts that people possess beyond verbal and mathematical, the two gifts or aptitudes normally evaluated and promoted in educational tests.

1. Using Gardner's list, identify the top two or three "intelligences" you possess and explain to the group why you chose them.

2. Using Gardner's list again, identify the top two or three "intelligences" possessed by a close friend or family member.

3. How can the realization that people may possess different intelligences help to make you a better servant-leader?

4. Assume that you are leading a group of people to build a house with Habitat for Humanity in an urban area. Also assume that among the group all of Gardner's multiple intelligences are represented. What tasks would you assign to the people who possess visual/spatial intelligence, verbal/linguistic intelligence, musical/rhythmical intelligence, and so on? Try to assign tasks to people from all seven categories of intelligence.

Read

An appreciation for the various intellectual abilities and multiple gifts people might bring to a task can also be fostered by reading 1 Corinthians 12:4–27. In these verses Saint Paul stresses the interrelatedness of the members of the Church and warns against esteeming one person's gift over the gifts of others. A servant-leader recognizes and values the diverse abilities of people in order to winsomely persuade them to action. It is equally important for the servant-leader to convince the people who follow his lead that all of their co-workers have gifts and talents necessary to complete the task. Read the following verses from First Corinthians as paraphrased in the *Living Bible*:

> 4 Now God gives us many kinds of special abilities, but it is the same Holy Spirit who is the source of them all. 5 There are different kinds of service to God, but it is the same Lord we are serving. 6 There are many ways in which God works in our lives, but it is the same God who does the work in and through all of us who are His. 7 The Holy Spirit displays God's power through each of us as a means of helping the entire church.
> 8 To one person the Spirit gives the ability to give wise advice; someone else may be especially good at studying and teaching, and this is his gift from the same Spirit. 9 He gives special faith to another, and to someone else the power to heal the sick. 10 He gives power for doing miracles to some, and to others power to prophesy and preach. He gives someone else the power to know whether evil spirits

are speaking through those who claim to be giving God's messages—or whether it is really the Spirit of God who is speaking. Still another person is able to speak in languages he never learned; and others, who do not know the language either, are given power to understand what he is saying. 11 It is the same Holy Spirit who gives all these gifts and powers, deciding which each one of us should have.

12 Our bodies have many parts, but the many parts make up only one body when they are all put together. So it is with the "body" of Christ. 13 Each of us is a part of the one body of Christ. Some of us are Jews, some are Gentiles, some are slaves, and some are free. But the Holy Spirit has fitted us all together into one body. We have been baptized into Christ's body by the one Spirit, and have all been given that same Holy Spirit.

14 Yes, the body has many parts, not just one part. 15 If the foot says, "I am not a part of the body because I am not a hand," that does not make it any less a part of the body. 16 And what would you think if you heard an ear say, "I am not part of the body because I am only an ear, and not an eye"? Would that make it any less a part of the body? 17 Suppose the whole body were an eye—then how would you hear? Or if our whole body were just one big ear, how could you smell anything?

18 But that isn't the way God has made us. He has made many parts for our bodies and has put each part just where He wants it. 19 What a strange thing a body would be if it had only one part! 20 So He has made many parts, but still there in only one body.

21 The eye can never say to the hand, "I don't need you." The head can't say to the feet, "I don't need you."

22 And some of the parts that seem weakest and least important are really the most necessary. 23 Yes, we are especially glad to have some parts that seem rather odd! And we carefully protect from the eyes of others those parts that should not be seen, 24 while of course the parts that may be seen do not require this special care. So God has put the body together in such a way that extra honor and care are given to those parts that might otherwise seem less important. 25 This makes for happiness among the parts, so that the parts have the same care for each other that they do for themselves. 26 If one part suffers, all parts suffer with it, and if one part is honored, all the parts are glad.

27 Now here is what I am trying to say: All of you together are the one body of Christ and each one of you is a separate and necessary part of it.

React

1. Verses 4–6 speak of the diversity of people in the church at Corinth, and also about the unity they share. What general examples of diversity were evident in the church? What unified each member in the church?

2. List the specific gifts given to the Corinthians enumerated in verses 4–10. According to verse 11, what should a servant-leader remember about the source and about the appropriateness of the gifts given to each person involved in a task?

3. What are the lessons Saint Paul is trying to convey to the Corinthians in his comparison of the church to a human body?

4. Recall a recent successful project in which you and others were involved and describe how the distinctive talents of each participant contributed to the effective completion of the project.

Read

An integral part of winsome persuasion is the constant encouragement of coworkers as they go about their meaningful tasks. The words of Hebrews 12:24 provide a directive to the servant-leader in his relationship with those he wishes to lead: "And let us consider how we may spur one another on toward love and good deeds." Spurring on or encouraging others to work together for the greater good is certainly central to successful servant-leadership. In fact, spurring on and encouraging are two leadership activities that are quite easy to do, easy, that is, if the servant-leader truly appreciates the varied gifts and abilities of all those working with him to complete a task.

REACT

1. Who is the most encouraging person you know? Why?

2. Recall a time when you received meaningful encouragement from someone in authority.

3. Recall a time when you provided meaningful encouragement to someone over whom you had authority.

4. From your own experience explain why encouragement can be such a powerful motivator.

RESPOND

As you grow in exercising servant-leadership this week, consider the following as you interact with coworkers, employees, friends, or family members:

A. Winsome persuasiveness is usually more effective than coercion.

B. The cultivation of sincere friendship is better than the declaration of logical arguments when it comes to persuading someone to do something.

C. Meaningful activity is centered in service to others.

D. Respect for the diverse gifts and abilities of others leads to the sincere appreciation of others.

E. All believers are members of the body of Christ, and each one is a separate and necessary part of it.

F. Encouragement empowers people to serve others.

4 Vision and the Servant-Leader

Ready

An effective servant-leader has the ability to formulate and communicate a vision that embodies the best values of the community he wishes to serve. Because a stated vision is based on the shared values of a community, members of the community tend to rally around the leader who articulates those values most clearly. However, before the servant-leader can articulate an effective vision, he must either listen to members of a community to determine their shared values, or he must remind the community of their core values that may have been unexpressed or repressed for a length of time.

Effective leaders, then, do not formulate vision statements in a vacuum, but instead remind people of the values they share and unite them in a cause. Visionary leaders articulate those values that hold both large and small communities together, and they help communities formulate goals and plans that dissolve divisions among community members and unite and inspire them to give their best efforts for the good of the whole group.

Choose one of the following visionary leaders, and describe the shared vision that the leader articulated for his community:

Moses

Abraham Lincoln

Winston Churchill

Martin Luther King Jr.

From your own experience, recall and then describe a visionary statement made by a leader that expressed the values shared by your own community and stirred your community to action. Define "community" broadly enough to include family, team, school, church, group, town, country, and so on.

40

Read

President Abraham Lincoln in a speech delivered in 1863 at the dedication of the Gettysburg National Cemetery during the height of the American Civil War made one of the most famous and effective vision statements in American history. Read what has become known as Lincoln's "Gettysburg Address":

Fourscore and seven years ago our fathers brought forth on this continent, a new nation, conceived in Liberty, and dedicated to the proposition that all men are created equal.

Now we are engaged in a great civil war, testing whether that nation or any nation so conceived and so dedicated, can long endure. We are met on a great battle-field of that war. We have come to dedicate a portion of that field, as a final resting place for those who here gave their lives that that nation might live. It is altogether fitting and proper that we should do this.

But, in a larger sense, we cannot dedicate—we cannot consecrate—we cannot hallow—this ground. The brave men, living and dead, who struggled here, have consecrated it far above our poor power to add or detract. The world will little note nor long remember what we say here, but it can never forget what they did here. It is for us, the living, rather to be dedicated here to the unfinished work which they who fought here have thus far so nobly advanced. It is rather for us to be here dedicated to the great task remaining before us—that from these honored dead we take increased devotion to that cause for which they gave the last full measure of devotion; that we here highly resolve that these dead shall not have died in vain; that this nation, under God, shall have a new birth of freedom; and that government of the people, by the people, for the people, shall not perish from the earth.

React

1. What shared values of his listeners does Lincoln state in his first sentence?

2. What "great task" does Lincoln ask his listeners to complete?

3. Suggest a one-sentence vision statement around which contemporary Americans might rally to solve a problem of the late 20th century.

Read

On January 19, 1998, a visionary Christian businessman named Rod Grimm died at the age of 51 in Bakersfield, California. Read excerpts from the article about Rod Grimm's visionary servant-leadership which appeared on the front page of the January 20, 1998, edition of the *Bakersfield Californian*:

Rod Grimm Succumbs to Cancer
by Robert Price

Rod Grimm, a straight-talking visionary who helped revolutionize the world carrot industry and in the process earned the admiration of employees, customers and colleagues, died Monday evening from cancer.

Grimm, president of Grimmway Farms, the world's No. 1 carrot producer and Kern County's top employer, was 51. ...

Although Grimm's death leaves a void at the top of an innovative, aggressive company, it is the loss of a friend, mentor and confidante that colleagues are mourning today.

"I never met a fairer man, or a smarter one," said Jon Tkac, whose company, U.S. Irrigation, has performed contract work for Grimmway.

"Rod did so much for so many," Tkac said. "Along with my father, he's my idol."

"They don't come any better," said Chuck Kirschenmann, a Lamont grower. "He was a visionary. He was always looking down the road to see where things should go. He was an idea man."

Grimm and his younger brother Bob, the company's 46-year-old vice president, came to Bakersfield from the Los Angeles area 17 years ago and within a decade had built a formidable enterprise in the productive fields at the southern edge of the valley.

Today, their $300 million company employs 3,600 workers and represents a major force in the economies of Lamont and Arvin, farm communities just south of Bakersfield.

42

The brothers, the two youngest of Herb and Sue Grimm's four children, were raised on their grandfather's chicken ranch in Anaheim and their parents' orange groves in Riverside County. The boys worked on the farm seven days a week.

Rod and Bob Grimm struck out together in the mid-1960s with five acres of sweet corn on their grandfather's farm. Rod was in college, Bob in the eighth grade. They hired their cousins and two sisters to sell the corn in roadside produce stands, and the enterprise grew from there.

In May 1981, after a series of disasters and triumphs, including a promising foray into Kern County carrot farming five years earlier, the brothers ... moved their operation to the San Joaquin Valley.

In January 1991, Grimmway Farms bought Belridge Farms, the nation's No. 4 carrot packer. In June 1995, Grimmway bought Mike Yurosek & Son, the nation's No. 2 carrot packer to [become] the industry leader with 50 to 55 percent of the California carrot market. ...

Rod Grimm, a fitness buff who cut a trim, muscular figure thanks to regular running and weight lifting, thrived on the competition.

"Competition is healthy," he said in a 1997 interview. "It's good competition that keeps you on your toes. It's called free enterprise, and no other system in the world works as well."

But Grimm measured success, he once said, "not just ... by money in the bank, but by job satisfaction and reward."

Grimm was well regarded by his employees, in part because of his determination that no question or grievance be ignored. He and his brother instituted a regular series of talk-back sessions with the Grimmway rank-and-file, and a number of new programs and policies, including an enhanced medical plan, resulted.

Grimm explained his philosophy, equally applicable in business and personal dealings, in his 1997 interview: "Do what you say you're going to do, and treat people the way you want to be treated."

Rod Grimm was so well regarded by employees that in August 1995 Kern's Punjab-speaking community—well represented in the Grimmway family—dressed him in a flowing yellow robe and honored him at a public ceremony at the Sikhs' Guru Ram Das Academy on Weedpatch Highway.

Grimm himself was a committed Christian who

attended and supported St. John's Lutheran Church in Bakersfield, among other institutions. He was not one to preach, preferring to demonstrate his faith by example.

"When you start talking about God, it starts to take on a feel like you're different from other people, like you're putting yourself on a pedestal," Grimm said. "We believe that we've been blessed by Him, but not because of what we have done, not because we've deserved it or led some kind of better life. It isn't what you've done. It's what He's done."

Grimm, through his company, did a lot for the communities of which Grimmway is so much a part.

Grimmway participated regularly in Lamont's annual economic summit conference and helped pay for numerous community projects, including the Arvin and Lamont libraries.

(Price, Robert. "Rod Grimm Succumbs to Cancer," *Bakersfield Californian*, 30 January 1998.)

REACT

1. How was Rod Grimm's visionary servant-leadership exemplified in the way that he and his brother treated their employees?

2. The article mentions Rod Grimm's support for church and community projects. Rod Grimm and his family also generously supported a number of other causes. Among them a program to train ethnic pastors to minister to different ethnic populations in America; an orphanage in Ensenada, Baja California, Mexico; a college scholarship program for children of Grimmway employees; and Christian higher education. How does the support of these causes reveal the visionary thinking of Rod Grimm and his family?

3. What do you think Rod Grimm meant when he said, "We Christians believe that we've been blessed by Him, but not because of what we have done, not because we've deserved it or led some kind of better life. It isn't what you've done. It's what He's done"?

44

Read

We now turn our attention to Nehemiah, a visionary servant-leader of God's people of the Old Testament. Before we read about Nehemiah's leadership, let's review the historical backdrop of Nehemiah's story.

Ancient Israel enjoyed its greatest years during King David's 40-year reign about 1000 years before the birth of Christ. Under David, Israel became a major military power and enjoyed a significant reputation among surrounding nations. However, under Solomon, David's son and successor, a split developed in Israel's military ranks, and Israel became a divided nation. Ten of Israel's 12 tribes moved to the north and established the so-called Northern Kingdom. Two tribes moved south, settled in Jerusalem and surrounding areas, and became known as Judah.

The kingdom remained divided for about 200 years until the Assyrians invaded the Northern Kingdom in 722 B.C. Some people fled south to Judah, but with the Assyrian invasion, the Northern Kingdom ceased to exist.

The land of Judah remained a Jewish nation until 586 B.C., when the Babylonians under King Nebuchadnezzar invaded Jerusalem. The Babylonians burned the temple, destroyed the wall around Jerusalem, and took the people captive. While the Jews were in captivity in Babylon, the Babylonians were defeated by the Medes and Persians. Cyrus, the king of Persia, looked favorably on the Jews and, about 70 years after the destruction of Jerusalem, he allowed the first group of exiles to return under a man named Zerubbabel. Years later a second group under the leadership of Ezra also returned to Jerusalem, and then a few years later, while Artaxerxes was king of Media-Persia, Nehemiah led a third group of Jewish people back to Jerusalem.

Read a retelling of Part I of Nehemiah's story found in *The Book of God* by Walter Wangerin Jr.:

> The name of the cupbearer of Artaxerxes I, king of Persia, is Nehemiah the son of Hacaliah. Nehemiah serves the king at his palace in Susa, two hundred miles east of Babylon. He is the king's intimate, both guarding and administering the royal apartments. He rose to such high office not by false arrogance and flattery, but by a talent for pragmatism and a faith in his own convictions.

Nehemiah is a eunuch. As cupbearer, he is completely committed to the king and reliable.

He is also a Jew, a worshiper of the great and terrible God. Nehemiah may have lived his whole life in the capital city of Persia. He may serve the Persian government as righteously as any citizen. Certainly, he is respected by the king of Persia himself. But Nehemiah is not Persian.

This is becoming more and more apparent to the king, because his cupbearer is growing disheveled.

It's spring. The rainy season is over. Artaxerxes has just returned from his winter palace in Babylon, specifically to enjoy the luxuriant flowering of Susa, soft in the mornings, pleasant in green evenings. And now the king has finished a satisfying meal. "Wine," he calls. Artaxerxes is sitting on a private terrace with the queen, Damaspia. When he looks up to greet his cupbearer bringing the wine, he sees a man unkempt and distracted. But Nehemiah has always been fastidious in his personal grooming.

"Nehemiah, what's the matter with you?" the king says. "Are you sick?"

Damaspia also looks up.

"No."

"You didn't wash! Damaspia, our good friend is filthy! Have you ever known him to fail his person or his office before?"

But the queen touches the king's wrist. "Softly," she says, gazing at Nehemiah. "This isn't a trespass. This is sadness of the heart."

Artaxerxes frowns at the cupbearer. "Are you sad, Nehemiah?"

"Yes."

"Why? Damaspia, do you know why he's sad?"

The queen holds her peace. Nehemiah stands still for a moment, then he speaks.

"Let the king live forever!" he says. "Why shouldn't my face be sad when the city, the place of my fathers' graves, lies waste, its walls broken and its gates burned with fire?"

"You mean Jerusalem?"

"Jerusalem. The City of David. Yes."

"But this isn't news. Jerusalem was destroyed a hundred and thirty years ago. Why does that depress you now?"

All at once the words pour from Nehemiah. He keeps his body erect, neither shaking nor spilling wine. But passion turns his tongue into a sword.

"Three months ago my brother Hanani came from Judah to Susa, and I asked him concerning the Jews still surviving in Jerusalem. He shook his head. My brother seemed almost to collapse. 'Trouble,' he said, 'great trouble and shame.' I questioned him all night long until I heard the whole of it, and I learned that my kin had tried to rebuild the walls of Jerusalem. They are harassed by Edomites and Samaritans and nomads and Arabians. They tried to protect themselves with a wall. A wall, my lord! What city of the least value can exist without a wall? But the governor of Samaria applied to the satrap above him, and that man received orders from your servants here in Susa commanding in your name that the Jews must stop building their wall. So the nobles of Samaria came and broke down the work my brother and my people had done. Broke the dressed stones. Broke the hope of the Jews who live in Jerusalem. Broke them."

Nehemiah closes his mouth and remains rigid for a moment, then steps forward and begins to pour the wine.

Softly, King Artaxerxes says, "Cupbearer, make a request of me."

Nehemiah straightens, glances toward the queen, who nods, then turns his face away and starts to whisper. He is whispering aloud, but in Hebrew. He is rocking slightly back and forth. He is praying.

Then, hawklike, he turns back to the king and says, "If it pleases the king, and if your servant has found favor in your sight, send me to Judah, to the city of my fathers' graves, that I might rebuild it."

"Send you to Judah?" Artaxerxes says. "Where would I get another cupbearer like—" But Queen Damaspia touches the king's wrist again, and he falls silent. Finally, he says, "How long will you be gone? When will you return?"

Nehemiah now speaks with pragmatic calculation. "It will take me four years to gather materials and to get there. Would you, my lord, let letters of safe passage be given me for the governors of the satrap beyond the River?—and a letter to Asaph, the keeper of the king's forest, permitting me to take timber for the beams of the gates and the fortress of the temple, for the wall of the city, and for the house I will occupy?"

The king nods, but tips his head toward the queen. "Evidently, Damaspia, our good friend has given the matter a great deal of thought. Did he know my answer before I did?"

Neither the queen nor the cupbearer speaks.

"And he is aware, of course," says the king, narrowing his eyes, "that he's asking the king of Persia to reverse a regal decree."

Nehemiah's face pales. Artaxerxes sees real fear there, but honors the decorum and the courage of the Jew who does not tremble, but continues stout and straight.

Suddenly the king smiles and leans back in his seat. "Four years to get there, Nehemiah? So how long will you be gone? When will you return?"

Though his face is still fixed in fear, Nehemiah swallows and presses forward. "There is one other request," he says, "that the king designate Judah a province of its own, separate from Samaria, and that he appoint me its first governor. In that case, my lord, I would be gone another twelve years. Sixteen years altogether."

Artaxerxes, king of Persia, almost laughs. "Jew, you are a wonder!" He reaches for his cup of wine, raises it to his lips, closes his eyes, and drinks the entire draught.

"It is a delicious spring, don't you think so, Damaspia?" He takes the queen's hand and lays it against his cheek, then to his cupbearer he says, "Wash your face, Nehemiah. Go. Save your city and govern your province with my blessing."

(Wangerin, *The Book of God,* 510–13)

REACT

1. What personal characteristics contributed to Nehemiah's ability to become a visionary servant-leader?

2. What shared vision of his community does Nehemiah express to King Artaxerxes?

3. Why do you think King Artaxerxes allowed Nehemiah to go to Jerusalem to rebuild its walls and govern it?

Read

Now read a retelling of Part II of Nehemiah's story by Walter Wangerin Jr.:

Nehemiah has been in Jerusalem for three days. On the first day he visited his brother Hanani. On the second he honored the sepulchers of the ancestors. Though he arrived with a Persian retinue over whom he has clear authority, he's told no one what he plans to do for Jerusalem. There is good reason for secrecy and for haste.

Now it is the night of the third day. The moon is full, the air chilly. Nehemiah, wrapped in a woolen robe, has ridden a mule to the ruins of the Valley Gate on the southwestern corner of Jerusalem. There he sits outside the gate above the valley of the son of Hinnom, gazing at broken stone and old char, murmuring softly to himself. He's calculating the job before him.

Two men walk through the fallen gate and join him. "I looked at the north side when I arrived," Nehemiah says. "We'll begin construction there, with the Sheep Gate westward to the Tower of the Hundred and the Tower of Hananel. Then we'll work in a circle against the sun. But this," Nehemiah sighs into the cold night wind. "This."

He urges the mule eastward on the rough ground outside the city— stones cracked and shaggy with weak, sudden falls of loose rock down into the valley on his right— until the columns of another old gate appear in the moonlight.

Nehemiah stops. "The Potsherd Gate," he whispers. "One hundred and seventy-five years ago the prophet stood here and said, *O kings of Judah, I am bringing such evil upon this place that the ears of every one who hears of it will tingle.* Ah, Jeremiah!"

Nehemiah dismounts and whispers again calculations of weight and materials, workers and time, then moves slowly onward.

It is midnight. Nehemiah has inspected the broken wall from the Potsherd Gate to the Fountain Gate, both burned by fire, and now he sees Gihon. Down below in the Kidron Valley is the spring and the long well-tunnel by which David sent his general Joab up into the city to storm it from within, terrifying the inhabitants, destroying their will in a single maneuver. Nehemiah heaves a deep sigh. So much happened between the young, joyful days of David and the Lamentations of the prophet Jeremiah.

But Nehemiah can't continue reminiscing. He has a

49

job to do. Besides, they've come to a point where the Kidron Valley drops straight down. The path disappears. Nehemiah whispers to the men behind him, "Enough," then backs his mule to a broader place and returns the way he came.

(Ibid., 513–14)

REACT

1. Visionary leaders are often accused of being unrealistic and impractical. In what very pragmatic activity does Nehemiah engage before he fully reveals his vision?

2. Although essentially pragmatic, what continues to motivate Nehemiah to carry out his plans?

READ

Read a portion of Part III of Nehemiah's story as retold by Walter Wangerin Jr.:

Sanballat, governor of the province of Samaria, is furious. He strides through the rooms of his administration, throwing his arms up and shouting. "It's bad enough that Judah should be snatched from me. I can't dispute the laws of the Medes and the Persians. But I *should* be able to control this lisping fool, this upstart in Jerusalem. What did you say he's gotten the Jews to do?"

Tobiah the Ammonite, a rich man from an old and prominent family, is following the governor from room to room, puffing because of his weight. "They're trying to build the walls of the city."

"How long have they been at it?"

"Three weeks."

"With success?"

"Well, the family of Eliashib the high priest has reconstructed the Sheep Gate. It's already been consecrated—"

"Ohhh!" Sanballat cries.

"—and the sons of Hassenaah have laid the beams of the Fish Gate and set its doors, its bolts, its bars—"

"This is too much!"

"Between the gates, the fortress protecting the north side of the temple is right now being—"

"What's the man's name?"

"Nehemiah."

Sanballat strides down the hall and out of his house, to an open yard where the captains of his troops are waiting. There, too, certain allies have gathered from territories surrounding Judah.

"What are these feeble Jews doing!" Sanballat bellows. "Can anyone estimate?—*will* they be able to restore things? Do they plan only to sacrifice? Will they finish this dream in a day? Will they revive the stones from heaps of rubbish? Can they make a wall of burned materials?"

Tobiah follows Sanballat into the yard, chuckling to himself. "Don't worry, my lord!" he calls. "What they are building—if a fox bumps the new wall, he'll break it down."

The captains laugh.

Sanballat, not laughing, turns to Tobiah. "Did you actually talk with this man Nehemiah?"

"I did," Tobiah says. "Geshem the Arab and I went together to Jerusalem. We met Nehemiah in a dirty marketplace. A beardless fellow. Scented and coiffed like a courtier. We said, 'What is this thing you're doing? Are you rebelling against the king?' He answered with religious haughtiness: 'God will make us prosper. But you have no portion in Jerusalem.' I started to laugh. I couldn't help it. The stinking marketplace, this Persian Jewish foppish eunuch surrounded by grim citizens of no country. Oh, I was tickled by the irony. But the fellow turned white and raised his voice and cursed me. *Oh God,* he cried, *turn their taunt back on their own heads.*"

"That's it!" Sanballat shouts. "Let's send the eunuch home!" All at once the governor of Samaria is raining commands upon his allies: "Geshem and the Arabians, attack from the south. Tobiah, go up with your forces from the northeast. Men of Ashod, cut straight in from the west. I'm going to hit the city at the north. I swear to burn the Sheep Gate and the Fish Gate and make a smoke of new timber. Move! Move, while there's no wall to stop us!"

In Jerusalem the burden-bearers have begun to fail. For fifty-two days they've carried dressed stone to workers on the wall, and now they stagger beneath their loads. The wall is only half built—a low girdling of stone around the city. They can't stop now, not even for a rest.

But all in one day alone seven reports have come from villages near the cities of Samaria that the enemies of

Jerusalem are preparing for military action. It is evening. Jews are watching the hills for the least movement. "They're coming to kill us," the weary people whisper, "and we have nothing to stop them. Nothing."

Suddenly a trumpet cuts the air above the city, and there stands the little governor from Susa at the top of the Tower of the Hundred, a torch in his right hand, his face bright with flame.

"Do not be afraid of them," Nehemiah cries to Jerusalem. "Remember the Lord, who is great and terrible, and fight for your brothers, your sons and daughters, your wives, and your homes!"

The citizens are not persuaded. "We have never fought before!" they yell. "And you are no captain!"

"But the Lord is! And I am his servant. Listen," cried Nehemiah, having measured the enemy and calculated the potential of his own people: "Here are our stratagems. First, let all the Jews of the villages nearby stay in the city night and day. We'll fill Jerusalem. Second, dig a ditch behind the wall, then station yourselves according to families in that trench with swords and spears and bows. Third, since you will be spread out from one another, listen for the trumpet, then rally to the place where the trumpet is. That's where the enemy will be attacking. Fourth, know this and believe it and let your hearts be fortified by it: *Our God will fight for us!*"

Whether the people trust Nehemiah or not, at least they have jobs for the evening and plans for tomorrow. This is new. In Judah there is purpose and encouragement. Yes, and hope. All night long the Jews dig a fine trench. In the morning, Nehemiah divides the working crew into two shifts, one to work and one to watch as long as work on the wall continues. Both day and night, then, there is always a show of force, spears moving back and forth within the city, men crying commands and salutations one to another.

(Ibid., 514–17)

REACT

1. How did Nehemiah persuade his dubious countrymen to follow his plan to defend Jerusalem against attack?

2. According to the story, the Jewish people were filled with "purpose, encouragement, and hope" as they prepared to defend Jerusalem. How does a visionary servant-leader fill people with "purpose, encouragement, and hope"?

3. Who is the ultimate source of Nehemiah's visionary leadership? Who is the ultimate source of the people filled with "purpose, encouragement, and hope"?

Read

Read the final section of Nehemiah as retold by Walter Wangerin Jr.:

> And now a new day dawns, cloudless, blue, and beautiful. There has not been such a day in Judah for more than two hundred years. Jerusalem is filled with people from the countryside, even from as far as the plains of the Jordan. They have all dressed with care, but some stand out like white lilies in a field of darker colors. These are wearing clean linen and carrying the instruments of gladness and thanksgiving and singing.
>
> The Levites are here, mingling among Jews, the children of Judah. They've brought their cymbals, their harps, and their lyres.
>
> And the sons of the singers are here.
>
> The city is alive with motion and laughter. Those still arriving pause to touch the new gates, each one shining wood, a sure protection for Zion against her enemies, calm glory, jewels in the crown of Jerusalem. Who can express what consolation the completion of the wall has caused in Jewish hearts?
>
> A trumpet unfurls its bright sound across the sky. People turn this way and that to find its source, and then they begin to stream toward the southwest, to the Valley Gate where the priests await them in the yard before the gate, and the governor stands on the ramparts above it.
>
> As the crowd swells all in that one place, the priests shake over them a mist of blood. The blood of sacrifice set-

tles like a red breath on the heads of the people. The priests themselves and the Levites have spent the last three days fasting for their personal purification. At the same time they offered sacrifices for the purification of the wall and the gates and the people. Now they are about to dedicate this new thing to the Lord.

"Sing!" cries Nehemiah—whose garments glitter with an orient glory. Dapper Nehemiah, cupbearer to a king—he has built a wall with faith and ferocity!

"Sing!" he cries. "Here at this gate we will divide into two great companies, each to walk the city wall in opposite directions. You praise-singing choirs, split and go first, half to the right, toward the Potsherd Gate, and half with me to the left. Let each half be followed by the leaders of Judah, then seven priests, then eight Levites. And sing! Let there be music from two sides as we walk the wall around, begging the protection of the Lord, giving thanks unto our God!"

And so the people of Judah rise up and walk on the fresh walls of Jerusalem. It is as if a fire has been ignited at the Valley Gate. From there the burning goes in two directions—each with the clashing of cymbals and the sharp strumming of taut string, with full-throated human song and individual shouts of praise: the people process on the top of the wall like bright flame, until the city is surrounded and all the women and the children are clapping and laughing along.

In this way the dedication is accomplished.

Then the two companies descend the wall, one at the Horse Gate south of the temple, one at the Sheep Gate north of it. So they meet again in the courts of the Lord, and there they offer sacrifices, Judah celebrating with a meal of union—for the Lord God has granted them a very great joy. Even at night the celebrations continue in Jerusalem with such gladness that their voices are heard north and south, in Samaria and in Edom. God is with the children of Judah. God is with Jacob again.

(Ibid., 520–22)

REACT

1. Where do the people give thanks to their God—not to Nehemiah, their servant-leader—for the completion of the wall around Jerusalem?

2. You too have been given by God a purpose—a vision. For many of you this was given by God when He chose you to be His own through Holy Baptism as a child. For others God provided you purpose—a vision—later in life as the Holy Spirit working through the Good News of Jesus Christ created saving faith in your heart. "But you are a chosen people, a royal priesthood, a holy nation, a people belonging to God, that you may declare the praises of Him who called you out of darkness into His wonderful light" (1 Peter 2:9). By grace through faith God has transformed you into a leader with vision. What does Peter describe as your purpose? How can and do you live out this purpose?

3. Review the definition of a visionary leader from the first pages of this chapter. How can you, one whom God has chosen to receive the blessings of faith—forgiveness of sins and eternal life through Jesus' death on the cross, articulate the values of God? Help unite members of your congregation to accomplish God's will and purpose—to share Jesus' love with everyone, everywhere.

Respond

This week encourage your family members, coworkers, or employees to recommit themselves to God and His Word through which their lives receive meaning and purpose.

5 Empathy and the Servant-Leader

Ready

True servant-leadership is impossible without empathy for one's family members, coworkers, or employees. And an empathetic, gracious spirit is impossible to cultivate unless a leader is willing to suspend his natural tendency toward self-centeredness. True release from self-centeredness is, of course, a gift from God through the saving merits of Jesus Christ. Christ's empathy for us, His willingness to take human form, to suffer and die for us, secured for us our salvation and made our self-centered attempts to redeem ourselves unnecessary.

Even though complete release from self-centeredness is impossible to achieve this side of heaven, servant-leaders, motivated by Jesus' love, model the empathy Christ showed for us and our condition as we relate to those we wish to serve and lead.

Recall and describe a gracious, empathetic leader who you believe was effective because he or she was able to understand your challenges, fears, joys, and so forth. Think perhaps of a coach who had at one time been a player or performer, or any leader who had come up through the ranks.

Then recall a nonempathetic leader who was ineffective largely because he or she was unable to understand your situation. Here perhaps think of a leader who had no experience in the area he or she was trying to provide leadership.

Read

In the late 1950s a white journalist named John Howard Griffin attempted to become more empathetic to the plight of black Americans in the Deep South. With the help of a dermatologist, Griffin underwent a series of medical treatments and temporarily changed his skin color to black. For six weeks as a black man he hitchhiked and rode buses through Mississippi, Alabama, Louisiana, and Georgia looking for work. He kept a journal of his experiences and later published a summary of those experiences in *Black Like Me*, a book that went on to sell over 10 million copies worldwide.

Griffin's attempt to empathize with blacks in the Deep South had a profound effect on him and on many people of all races who have read his book. Read this excerpt from the first few pages of *Black Like Me*:

> For years the idea had haunted me, and that night it returned more insistently than ever.
> If a white man became a Negro in the Deep South, what adjustments would he have to make? What is it like to experience discrimination based on skin color, something over which one has no control?
> How else except by becoming a Negro could a white man hope to learn the truth? Though we lived side by side throughout the South, communication between the two races had simply ceased to exist. Neither really knew what went on with those of the other race. The Southern Negro will not tell the white man the truth. He long ago learned that if he speaks a truth unpleasing to the white, the white will make life miserable for him.
> The only way I could see to bridge the gap between us was to become a Negro. I decided I would do this.
> I prepared to walk into a life that appeared suddenly mysterious and frightening. With my decision to become a Negro I realized that I, a specialist in race issues, really knew nothing of the Negro's real problem.

(From Griffin, John Howard. *Black Like Me*. [New York: Penguin Books, 1960], 7–8)

REACT

1. Why did Griffin feel it was necessary for him to "become a Negro"?

2. Compare Griffin's decision to empathetic servant-leadership.

Read

Read these excerpts from *Black Like Me,* which describe the reaction Griffin received as a black man in the Deep South:

I went into a drugstore that I had patronized [as a white man] every day since my arrival. I walked to the cigarette counter where the same girl I had talked with every day waited on me.

"Package of Picayunes, please," I said in response to her blank look.

She handed them to me, took my bill and gave me change with no sign of recognition, none of the banter of previous days. (Ibid., 18)

Night was near when I finally caught the bus going toward town. Two blocks before Canal, the bus makes a left turn off Claiborne. I rang the bell to get off at this stop. The driver pulled to a halt and opened the door. He left it open until I reached it. I was ready to step off when the door banged shut in my face. Since he had to remain there waiting for a clear passage through traffic, I asked him to let me off.

"I can't leave the door open all night," he said impatiently.

He waited another full minute, but refused to open the door.

"Will you please let me off at the next corner, then?" I asked, controlling my temper, careful not to do or say anything that would jeopardize the Negroes' position in the area.

He did not answer. I returned to my seat. A woman watched me with sympathetic anger, as though she in no way approved of this kind of treatment. However, she did not speak.

At each stop, I sounded the buzzer, but the driver continued through the next two stops. He drove me eight blocks past my original stop and pulled up then only because some white passengers wanted to get off. I followed them to the front. He watched me, his hand on the lever that would spring the doors shut.

"May I get off now?" I asked quietly when the others had stepped down.

"Yeah, go ahead," he said finally, as though he had tired of the cat-and-mouse game. I got off, sick, wondering how I could ever walk those eight blocks back to my original stop.

In all fairness, I must add that this is the only example of deliberate cruelty I encountered on any of the city buses of New Orleans. Even though I was outraged, I knew he did not commit this indignity against me, but against my black flesh, my color. This was an individual act by an individual, and certainly not typical. (Ibid., 47–48)

In the bus station lobby, I looked for signs indicating a colored waiting room, but saw none. I walked up to the ticket counter. When the lady ticket-seller saw me, her otherwise attractive face turned sour, violently so. This look was so unexpected and so unprovoked I was taken aback.

"What do you want?" she snapped.

Taking care to pitch my voice to politeness, I asked about the next bus to Hattiesburg.

She answered rudely and glared at me with such loathing I knew I was receiving what the Negroes call "the hate stare." It was my first experience with it. It is far more than the look of disapproval one occasionally gets. This was so exaggeratedly hateful I would have been amused if I had not been so surprised.

I framed the words in my mind: "Pardon me, but have I done something to offend you?" But I realized I had done nothing—my color offended her.

"I'd like a one-way ticket to Hattiesburg, please," I said and placed a ten-dollar bill on the counter.

"I can't change that big a bill," she said abruptly and turned away, as though the matter were closed. I remained at the window, feeling strangely abandoned but not knowing what else to do. In a while she flew back at me, her face flushed, and fairly shouted: "I *told* you—I can't change that big a bill."

"Surely," I said stiffly, "in the entire Greyhound system there must be some means of changing a ten-dollar bill. Perhaps the manager—"

She jerked the bill furiously from my hand and stepped away from the window. In a moment she reappeared to hurl my change and the ticket on the counter with such force most of it fell on the floor at my feet. I was truly dumbfounded by this deep fury that possessed her whenever she looked at me. Her performance was so venomous, I felt sorry for her. It must have shown in my expression, for her face congested to high pink. She undoubtedly considered it a supreme insolence for a Negro to dare to feel sorry for her.

I stooped to pick up my change and ticket from the floor. I wondered how she would feel if she learned that the

Negro before whom she had behaved in such an unladylike manner was habitually a white man. (Ibid., 53–54)

I have held no brief for the Negro. I have looked diligently for all aspects of "inferiority" among them and I cannot find them. All the cherished question-begging epithets applied to the Negro race, and widely accepted as truth even by men of good will, simply prove untrue when one lives among them. This, of course, excludes the trash element, which is the same everywhere and is no more evident among Negroes than whites.

When all the talk, all the propaganda has been cut away, the criterion is nothing but the color of skin. My experience proved that. They judged me by no other quality. My skin was dark. That was sufficient reason for them to deny me those rights and freedoms without which life loses its significance and becomes a matter of little more than animal survival. (Ibid., 114)

I developed a technique of zigzagging back and forth. In my bag I kept a damp sponge, dyes, cleansing cream and Kleenex. It was hazardous, but it was the only way to transverse an area both as Negro and white. As I traveled, I would find an isolated spot, perhaps an alley at night or the brush beside a highway, and quickly apply the dye to face, hands and legs, then rub off and reapply until it was firmly anchored in my pores. I would go through the area as a Negro and then, usually at night, remove the dyes with cleansing cream and tissues and pass through the same area as a white man.

I was the same man, whether white or black. Yet when I was white, I received the brotherly-love smiles and the privileges from whites and the hate stares or obsequiousness from the Negroes. And when I was a Negro, the whites judged me fit for the junk heap, while the Negroes treated me with great warmth. (Ibid., 124)

React

1. Choose one excerpt and describe how Griffin's experience helped make him more empathetic to the prejudice experienced by black men and women.

2. How did Griffin's experiences make him empathetic toward the negative effect that prejudice and racism had on the white people who were guilty of prejudicial behavior?

Read

Read the following essay by Kurt Krueger, written years after the events described took place. The author recalls the gracious, empathetic spirit of his father toward him when he was a teenager.

A Gracious Father

I have a true story to tell you about my father. Before I get into the story, let me tell you a little bit about him. Before he died a few years ago, he was a minister of the Gospel, a devoted husband, and the father of four children. He loved his Lord, his family, and the people in his congregation.

And, more to the point of this story, he loved everything associated with new automobiles. He loved the way new cars looked and smelled. He loved their smooth acceleration and stable cornering. He loved all the electric gismos that lowered the windows, that locked the doors, that scanned for radio stations, that dimmed the dashboard lights, that defrosted the windows, that moved the mirrors. In a sentence, my father loved new cars.

Because my father had this somewhat intense relationship with the automobile, an annual winter event in Milwaukee, Wisconsin, where we lived during my youth, turned into a family ritual, at least among the males in my family. That ritual involved attending the Auto Show held every February in the Civic Auditorium in downtown Milwaukee.

Perhaps my father took my two younger brothers and me downtown every February to look at the new cars because the smell of new auto upholstery and the sight of polished fenders somehow obliterated the gloom and gray of the long Milwaukee winters with the promise of Spring. Or perhaps the rainbow of colors and the cacophony of sounds which assaulted our senses when we first entered the auditorium overwhelmed us with their archetypal significance. Or maybe he just liked to be around new cars.

Anyway, for years, like clockwork, the four males in my family would dutifully and joyfully journey to the annual Auto Show where we would slam doors and kick tires and collect, in briefcase sized plastic bags, scores of new car brochures.

When we got a little older, my father often would go off by himself at the auto show to do some serious car shopping, while we three boys traded brochures or watched the female spokesmodels, mesmerized by their incoherent descriptions of suspension systems and hydraulic lifters.

When my father returned from his solo excursions to the land of Lincolns and Cadillacs, he sometimes had this far away look in his eyes which meant to us that he was thinking seriously of buying a new car that Spring; that is, if he could convince our mother of the wisdom of such a thought.

It surprised no one, then, that in the spring of 1963 my father bought a brand new, royal blue Pontiac Catalina with all the bells and whistles that General Motors could load into a new car.

Although this was the first car that I would learn to drive, and although this was the first car I would eventually crash, I was only 15 years old in 1963 and I didn't have my driver's license yet.

But my dad let me back the new car out of our garage and down the driveway as many times as I wanted, if I washed it every weekend. And that's what I did for weeks. I remember spending hours washing and detailing that new blue Pontiac. And it wasn't a small car. As the saying goes, a family of four could have slept in the trunk.

Anyway, I faithfully washed those royal blue fenders and polished the chrome bumpers and took the road tar off the rocker panels. Oh, yes, and I scrubbed the whitewall tires with SOS pads.

As you probably know SOS pads are made of steel wool, and will scrub the stain off of practically anything that can stand to be scrubbed by fibers of steel.

For some inexplicable reason, one Saturday afternoon in the Spring of 1963, after I scrubbed the whitewalls with an SOS pad, I took that pad of steel wool and proceeded to scrub the fenders, roof, trunk, and hood of my father's new, dark blue Pontiac Catalina.

I remember being amazed at how much dirt came off of the car, and I remember being even more amazed that most of the dirt was royal blue.

After I saw that the SOS pad had turned dark blue, I

hastily rinsed and dried the car, and when I looked closely at the car's finish, I saw hundreds and hundreds of circular scratches which had not been there before. It was painfully apparent that I had ruined the finish on my father's new car.

When my father walked home from church an hour or so later, I was still standing in the driveway hunched over the hood of the Pontiac, trying desperately to wax and polish the scratches away. But the scratches did not go away. Almost in tears when my father approached, I told him what I had done.

My father saw the scratches and saw how devastated and ashamed I was. And do you know what my father did? Do you know what my father, the man who got dreamy-eyed every year at the auto show, did to me that warm Spring day in Milwaukee? He put his arm on my shoulder and said, "That's all right, son. You didn't mean any harm. It's only a car. Don't worry about it."

That, my friends, is an example of Christian empathy. An example of understanding and undeserved grace. You see, my father was convinced—and this is what he taught me that day and on many other occasions—that because we have been forgiven and have the assurance of eternal life, we are free to forgive and to show empathy and to act graciously toward those among us who mess up.

As my father would have said in the Spring of 1963, "From the narrow perspective of today, scratching the paint on a new car is a foolish thing to do; but from the perspective of eternity, what do a few scratches on painted steel amount to?"

My story has a sequel. About two months after I SOS'd my dad's new car, our church youth group held a car wash. After each car was washed, we asked the owners if they wanted us to wax their car. After an entire morning of car washing, not one owner consented to the prospect of having 10 teenagers wax their car. My dad, however, finally gave his OK to us to wax his car. With much horsing around, as you can imagine, we got a coat of paste wax on the car and horsed around some more while the wax dried to a light sheen. Then, as one of the older kids began to polish the car, he noticed a lot of circular scratches in the dark blue paint and asked my dad so that all could hear, "Hey, pastor. How'd you get all these scratches on your new car?" My stomach sank into my shoes. I looked at my dad; my dad looked at me. Finally, my dad smiled, shrugged his shoulders, and said, "Let's finish up here."

My dad had the chance to nail me to the wall, to embarrass me in front of my friends, to proclaim that his stupid son had SOS'd his new car's finish beyond a dullness that no paste wax could ever redeem. But my dad said not one condemnatory word. He merely shrugged off the question and, in so doing, reaffirmed his forgiveness and his understanding of my situation.

My dad was indeed a gracious father, a father who understood, who freely forgave and did so because he believed in the One who understood and forgave him.

REACT

1. Why do you suppose the father was so understanding of his son's mistake?

2. What do you think the son learned about servant-leadership from his father as a result of his father's graciousness toward him?

3. Describe a time when you were able to put aside self-centeredness and to display an empathetic spirit toward someone who made a mistake.

Read

The miracles Jesus performed during His earthly ministry, particularly His healing miracles, reveal the empathy our Lord had toward the imperfect physical and spiritual condition of mankind. Christ's compassion for those in need led Him to help those in need. Christ's miracles teach us that empathy leads to action. An empathetic servant-leader must do more than feel compassion; he must use his feelings of compassion to speak words and perform works of compassion.

Read about two of Jesus' miracles of healing recorded in Matthew 9:18–26:

A Dead Girl and a Sick Woman

While He was saying this, a ruler came and knelt before Him and said, "My daughter has just died. But come and put Your hand on her, and she will live." Jesus got up and went with him, and so did His disciples.

Just then a woman who had been subject to bleeding for twelve years came up behind Him and touched the edge of His cloak. She said to herself, "If I only touch His cloak, I will be healed."

Jesus turned and saw her. "Take heart, daughter," He said, "your faith has healed you." And the woman was healed from that moment.

When Jesus entered the ruler's house and saw the flute players and the noisy crowd, He said, "Go away. The girl is not dead but asleep." But they laughed at Him. After the crowd had been put outside, He went back in and took the girl by the hand, and she got up. News of this spread through all that region.

React

1. As revealed in this reading, how did Jesus' reputation as a compassionate healer cause people to react?

2. It goes without saying that the dynamic between Jesus and the people who followed Him is different than the dynamic between contemporary servant-leaders and the people who follow them, for, unlike leaders today, Jesus had the power to perform miraculous healings and to bring people back from the dead. However, how might a contemporary, empathetic servant-leader also perform seemingly miraculous "healings" through words and actions of compassion?

3. A servant-leader is often called upon to show empathy to more than one person at a time. How did Jesus deal with multiple needs for compassion in this section of Scripture?

Read

Read about another healing miracle, found in Mark 10:46–52:

Blind Bartimaeus Receives His Sight

Then they came to Jericho. As Jesus and His disciples, together with a large crowd, were leaving the city, a blind man, Bartimaeus (that is, the Son of Timaeus), was sitting by the roadside begging. When he heard that it was Jesus of Nazareth, he began to shout, "Jesus, Son of David, have mercy on me!"

Many rebuked him and told him to be quiet, but he shouted all the more, "Son of David, have mercy on me!"

Jesus stopped and said, "Call him."

So they called to the blind man, "Cheer up! On your feet! He's calling you." Throwing his cloak aside, he jumped to his feet and came to Jesus.

"What do you want me to do for you?" Jesus asked him.

The blind man said, "Rabbi, I want to see."

"Go," said Jesus, "your faith has healed you." Immediately he received his sight and followed Jesus along the road.

React

1. What might this miracle teach us about a servant-leader's priorities?

2. How did Bartimaeus respond to Jesus' act of compassion? What lesson for the servant-leader is suggested by his response?

Read

If time permits read the following portions of Scripture, which record other miracles of healing, and note how Jesus responded to those in need and how those who were healed or witnessed the healing responded to Jesus:

A. Jesus heals Peter's mother-in-law (Matthew 8:14–15)
B. Jesus heals a paralytic (Mark 2:1–12)
C. Jesus heals a crippled woman (Luke 13:10–17)
D. Jesus heals the official's son (John 4:43–54)

Respond

Compassion and empathy cannot be faked, at least not for very long. Empathetic words and actions must be genuine and heart-felt, flowing from a true desire to understand and serve people. People who believe that their leader truly knows them and their circumstances and that he is willing to help them accomplish their tasks will readily follow his lead. And people who have received empathy and compassion from their leader will more readily show an empathetic and compassionate spirit toward others.

This week pay particular attention to a family member, coworker, or employee who seems to be struggling with some task or problem and look for ways (and then take the time!) to listen empathetically and to speak and act compassionately towards that person.

6 Humility and the Servant-Leader

Ready

People who achieve or are placed in positions of leadership must guard against the temptation to let their authority over others "go to their head." The temptation to abuse one's authority is probably more acute in hierarchical organizations than in democratic ones. But Lord Acton's assertion that "power tends to corrupt" is applicable to any situation in which one person has authority over another. A person in power must guard against slipping into an arrogance that may distort his personality and destroy his relationship with others, and that may eventually threaten the success of the entire enterprise that he leads. By definition, a servant-leader who becomes arrogant ceases to be a leader because his leadership depends on his commitment to others, not on his authority over those who look to him for leadership. A true servant-leader exhibits and practices a humility that keeps him focused on the well-being, growth, and success of others who ultimately receive praise for what he has empowered them to do.

In this chapter we will look at characteristics of humility as exhibited and practiced by servant-leaders, but before we do, begin by responding to the following:

1. Think of a person whose promotion to a leadership position led to an arrogance which tended to corrupt him or her. What specific behaviors were exhibited by this arrogant leader?

2. Think of a time when you let a leadership assignment "go to your head," a time when you became overly demanding or even dictatorial because you were put in charge.

3. Think of a leader who you admire because of his or her humble spirit who allowed others to receive the praise for the completion of a project or task.

4. Think of a time when you led a group of people to the successful completion of a task and then allowed them to receive acclamation for a job well done. Perhaps you can recall "biting your tongue" when someone praised a colleague or subordinate for doing something for which you had primary responsibility.

Read

The book of Proverbs contains many statements that express truths about human behavior and provide direction for successful living. A key statement in this Old Testament book is found in Proverbs 1:7: "The fear of the LORD is the beginning of knowledge, but fools despise wisdom and discipline."

That is, true knowledge and wisdom are based on fearing (respecting, honoring, worshiping, obeying) the Lord, but only the foolish despise the Lord and His instruction. Throughout the book, various proverbs speak about arrogance and about humility in an effort to instruct the reader about the dangers of pride and the rewards of a humble spirit. Proverbs 11:2, for example, speaks about both:

"When pride comes, then comes disgrace, but with humility comes wisdom."

Before we look at other proverbs that deal with arrogance and humility, react to Proverbs 11:2 by answering the questions below.

React

1. How might pride lead to disgrace? Can you think of any famous politicians, athletes, entertainers, or TV evangelists whose arrogance brought disgrace upon them or others?

2. How might a humble person be considered wise? Why might it be difficult to think of any people famous for their humility?

Read

Read the following three proverbs, which warn against arrogance and pride:

"To fear the LORD is to hate evil; I hate pride and arrogance, evil behavior and perverse speech" (Proverbs 8:13).

"Pride only breeds quarrels, but wisdom is found in those who take advice" (Proverbs 13:10).

"Pride goes before destruction, a haughty spirit before a fall" (Proverbs 16:18).

React

1. Note the words in these three proverbs that state or imply that a person's pride does not merely affect him but also affects those around him.

2. Notice that the word "pride" here means "arrogance," not "self-respect." What is the difference between "arrogance" and "self-respect"?

Read

Read the following proverbs, which praise humility, sometimes after condemning pride:

"The fear of the LORD teaches a man wisdom, and humility comes before honor" (Proverbs 15:33).

"Before his downfall a man's heart is proud, but humility comes before honor" (Proverbs 18:12).

"Humility and the fear of the LORD bring wealth and honor and life" (Proverbs 22:4).

"A man's pride brings him low, but a man of lowly spirit gains honor" (Proverbs 29:23).

70

React

1. Why is honor considered the end result of humility? How do you think the author of these verses would define honor?

2. How can humble servant-leaders attain honor?

Read

The following essay about Princeton University's basketball team is from the March 16, 1998, issue of *Time* magazine. It was written by Richard Stengle.

Stardom? They'd Rather Pass

I'm not a fan. I never root for one team over another because I generally don't care who wins. But I admit I do feel vindicated by the Princeton University basketball team's 26-and-1 record and its rank of No. 8 in the country. I confess I wouldn't be all that disappointed if the team wins a couple of games in the NCAA championships that start this week. But only because it might teach a lesson to the guys I play pickup basketball with on Tuesday nights.

I was a scrub, a sophomore backup guard, on the last great Princeton squad, the team that won the National Invitational Tournament in 1975. I can't take much credit for the victory, except that I did occasionally force the first team to work up a sweat in practice, and I did absorb my fair share of the coaches' abuse. But the real curse of a Princeton basketball education is that it renders you unfit for pickup games for the rest of your life. No one looks for the open man. No one sees you when you go backdoor. Guys hog the ball and force shots from 30 feet. My inner coach wants to bench all these Michael Jordan wannabes. But it's a lost cause. You see such play everywhere these days. Especially in the NBA.

The current Princeton team plays exactly the way my team did, with a few new wrinkles and some better athletes. My coach was the ornery philosopher Pete Carril.

Princeton's current coach, Bill Carmody, apprenticed under Carril for 14 years. Carril saw the 94-ft. by 54-ft. hard court as a moral playground where the cardinal virtue was unselfishness. The embodiment of unselfishness was the assist, the small act of grace of giving up the ball to a teammate who has a better shot. Check out the box score of a Princeton game: the team gets two-thirds of its baskets off assists, a rarity in this era of run-and-gun shooters who have eyes only for the hoop.

For the past 30 years, Princeton players have been bullied and brainwashed into looking for the pass first and the shot second. When the leather of the roundball touches your hands, your first thought is, Who else is open? Not, How am I gonna get my shot? It's not easy to learn, and it goes against the grain of me-first American individualism and the lure of million-dollar sneaker contracts. The highest skill of a Princeton basketball player is not to run, jump or shoot but to *see*. And it is still the rarest basketball skill of all.

Princeton is an anomaly not just because it starts five anonymous white guys in what has become a game of bigger-than-life black stars, but because in basketball today, individualism pays. Fans buy tickets to see darting one-on-one moves, awesome dunks and 30-point games by players with multimillion-dollar endorsement deals, not pinpoint bounce passes and pretty pick-and-rolls by a bunch of unknowns whose leading scorer is averaging under 15 points a game.

The real genius of the Princeton offense is not its moral idealism but its real-world practicality. At every moment you have a set of binary options that anticipates each possible move of your opponent—and gives you a way to overcome it. Is your man overplaying you? Cut backdoor. Is he sloughing off? Come out for the pass. If your teammate dribbles toward you, either cut away or scoot round for a hand-off. As if you were playing judo with a ball, you always use the strength of your opponent against him.

It just so happens that the Princeton offense, with its patient, intricate passing, is suited to the type of player who goes to school there: mostly kids who score at least 1,100 on their SATS, whose parents have houses with two-car garages, and who think about business school, not the NBA, after they graduate. It's a system designed for white boys who can't jump, though this year's team—which has beaten Texas, North Carolina State and Wake Forest and lost by only eight points to No.2-ranked North Carolina—has kids who can.

At the moment, the five Princeton starters not only have to carry a complicated offense around in their heads but must also bear the weight of being the moral dream team of out-of-shape editorial writers who see the Tigers as the antidote to all the greed and thuggery of big-time sports. But it's unfair to these kids to label them warriors of virtue in a venal world. I promise you, all they are thinking about is winning games, not winning hearts and minds.

But after they graduate, when they're taking depositions, not jump shots, and trying to keep away the paunch by playing in pickup games on weekends and evenings, they are going to find that they're playing a different game from everyone else on the court. Basketball is more than just a metaphor for who we are; we show who we are when we play it.

I've never bothered to try to explain to the guys I play with on Tuesday nights why I don't shoot more. Mainly, I'm just trying to get a workout and not get hurt, but I suppose on another level, I'm still looking for the open man.

(Stengei, Richard. "Stardom? They'd Rather Pass." *Time,* 16 March 1998, 82)

REACT

1. Why is the author frustrated by what he sees happening in much of collegiate and professional basketball today?

2. Why does the author praise the way the Princeton Tigers play the game of basketball?

3. Could Division I NCAA athletics and professional sports thrive, or even survive, in America without the arrogance of some players and coaches?

4. The author suggests that the way Princeton plays basketball has real-world practicality. How might always looking

to make an assist be a good real-world practice for a humble servant-leader to follow?

5. What are some of the forces that keep collegiate and professional basketball players from practicing humble behavior?

6. What are some of the forces that keep people in any occupation from practicing humble behavior?

Read

The story of another basketball team whose members have been praised for their uncommon humility comes from the 1998 NCAA basketball tournament. In the tournament, tiny Valparaiso University (3,500 students) of tiny Valparaiso, Indiana (25,000 people), beat two larger schools, Ole Miss and Florida State, to advance to the Sweet 16 round of the NCAA tournament where they eventually lost to Rhode Island. Along the way, however, the play and demeanor of Valpo's players impressed sports columnists and editorial writers across the nation. Read what some of these columnists and writers, as quoted in *VALPO*, the magazine of Valparaiso University, had to say about Valpo's basketball team:

Valpo Story Becoming a Fairy Tale

We need a university whose coach, Homer Drew, takes each of his potential recruits to the office of the president, Alan Harre, who proceeds to give them all the same speech: You won't be on television. You won't build a thick portfolio of adulatory clippings from the national press. You will, however, get a good education. You will get good coaching, with a minimum of screaming.

(From the *San Francisco Chronicle*, 20 March 1998)

Dale Brown, Homer Drew's boss at LSU 26 years ago and a man who took the lowest seed ever to the Final Four—his No. 11 LSU team in 1986—says Valpo can win, and must. "This is what college athletics should be, this

Valpo team," Brown said. "There's a purity there that the NCAA needs. It's a cleansing thing. Homer Drew represents all that's good in college athletics."

(From the *Post-Tribune* [Northwest Indiana], 20 March 1998)

Valpo and Values

What most distinguishes Valpo is not its amazing basketball team, but that it is one of a handful of higher education institutions trying to maintain high scholastic standards and Christian values in the face of pressure to become as secular and politically correct as the rest of the academic world. ... It's funny how success in sports can cause us to take note of an institution that was already distinguished, simply ignored and unappreciated by the secular world. It's funny how national TV exposure can jam the phone lines at a place already deserving of a good reputation.

(From the *Indianapolis Star*, 20 March 1998)

Even after losing, Valparaiso remains one of the tournament's biggest winners:

This bunch is a team in the best sense of the word; their achievements are greater than the sum of their parts. Remember them. In searching for a symbol of hope in some far-off tomorrow, remember them well. They came so unexpectedly. They touched us in a special way and reached a plateau that most will see only in their dreams.

(From *The State*, Columbia, S.C., 22 March 1998)

Valparaiso leaves a lasting image of class in victory and defeat:

They are wholesome, well-spoken student-athletes, all on track to earn degrees. There were no tattoos on their arms, chips on their shoulders or profanities in their vocabulary. From disparate backgrounds and abilities, they had become the essence of a team and of a family. Finally, their work and commitment had paid off in stunning success.

But it was in defeat that the real character of the Crusaders—and their fans—came to the fore. Few teams have ever bowed out with such dignity, grace and class.

In the news business, we always need to look ahead, not behind. But in the people business, we occasionally need to look back and find a Valparaiso there somewhere, offering inspiration, providing example.

Looking ahead, there will be a Final Four and an ultimate one. But in the years ahead, when I look back at the 1998 NCAA tournament, I'll think of Valpo.

(From the *Indianapolis Star,* 22 March 1998)

Rᴇᴀᴄᴛ

1. Why do you suppose Valpo's basketball team captured the hearts of so many sports fans in America during the 1998 NCAA tournament?

2. What character traits do a group of people exhibit working humbly to attain a goal or accomplish a task?

Rᴇᴀᴅ

One of the best statements on humility in the Bible is found in St. Paul's letter to the church at Philippi. From your own Bible, read the first 11 verses of Chapter 2 (titled "Imitating Christ's Humility" in the NIV) and then read the following paraphrase of Philippians 2:1–11 from the *Living Bible*:

> Is there any such thing as Christians cheering each other up? Do you love me enough to want to help me? Does it mean anything to you that we are brothers in the Lord, sharing the same Spirit? Are your hearts tender and sympathetic to all? Then make me truly happy by loving each other and agreeing wholeheartedly with each other, working together with one heart and mind and purpose.
>
> Don't be selfish; don't live to make a good impression on others. Be humble, thinking of others as better than yourself. Don't just think about your own affairs, but be interested in others, too, and in what they are doing.
>
> Your attitude should be the kind that was shown us by Jesus Christ, who, though he was God, did not demand and cling to his rights as God, but laid aside his mighty power and glory, taking the disguise of a slave and becoming like men. And he humbled himself even further, going so far as actually to die a criminal's death on a cross.
>
> Yet it was because of this that God raised him up to the heights of heaven and gave him a name which is above every other name, that at the name of Jesus every knee

shall bow in heaven and on earth and under the earth, and every tongue shall confess that Jesus Christ is Lord, to the glory of God the Father.

REACT

1. How did Jesus Christ humble Himself?

2. How did God the Father honor such humility?

3. According to the text, what are some of the things we can do or avoid doing as we are motivated by Jesus' love for us to imitate the humility exhibited by the servant-leadership of Jesus Christ?

4. Describe a time when a leader "humbled himself" to be of service to you or to others.

READ

The story of Gideon is about how an Old Testament leader was used by the Lord to humble and defeat the enemies of Israel. Before he became a leader Gideon was consumed by a cowardly self-centeredness, which rendered him powerless. However, once Gideon learned to humble himself to the will of the Lord, he became the courageous man who led his people to victory. Read the story of Gideon from Judges 6, 7, and 8 as retold by Walter Wangerin Jr. in his *The Book of God.*

GIDEON

The people of Israel did what was evil in the sight of the Lord.

A farmer named Joash, of the tribe of Manasseh, built an altar to Ba'al. He lived not more than twenty miles southwest of Mount Tabor. Beside the altar he erected a tall wooden pole upon which was carved the image of Asherah, swelling goddess of fertility. Joash still called on the name of the Lord; yet, at seedtime he also made judicious appeals to Ba'al and Asherah. So did most of his clan, the Abiezerites. So did many in Israel.

But just as the fields that had been planted under a pagan ritual grew ripe to the harvest, a wild desert people came riding from regions east of the Salt Sea. Midianites! They terrified Israel. Riding monsters as swift as the wind, they appeared at dawn, seized the fresh grain, trampled the standing crops, burned the fields, killed peasants from the backs of their impossible beasts, and disappeared again before the dusk.

Camels—they rode *camels!* They reached *down* to club the skulls of Israel. They covered more than sixty miles in a day. And they were able to bear enormous quantities of produce away, two hundred miles away. The distance once protected Israel. But Midian had learned to ride camels.

They returned the following year, again at the harvest. This time they slaughtered the livestock, too, leaving not a sheep nor an ox behind.

Next the Midianites came with their tents. Like locusts they swarmed over the Jordan, too many to count, feeding off the green land and driving many Israelites into the mountains to hide in caves and strongholds.

So it went for seven years.

And the people of Israel cried for help to the Lord.

One night, under cover of darkness, someone came and pulled down the altar which Joash the Abiezerite had built for Ba'al. In the morning people found the old stones scattered; but new stones had been laid to form another altar— upon which one of Joash's bulls had already been sacrificed. And the wood that burned the sacrifice was the pole of the image of Asherah. Her face had turned to ashes.

The people said to one another, "Who did this thing?"

Now one of the sons of Joash, Gideon, was threshing wheat in a square stone pit as deep as his chest.

This was his father's wine vat. In better times he would be singing here, roaring happy songs with other men as they trod the grapes, and as the sweet juice flowed down channels to lower, cooler vats. In better times he would be threshing grain on a high, open ground with the help of his ox and his children. For the ox would pull the threshing sledge while his children gave it weight and laughed while he led them round and round on piles of stalks, separating the hard, good kernel from the chaff.

But these were bad times. Midian might sweep down at any moment. Gideon was hiding. He was beating the stalks with a stick and a flail, threshing in the old way, crouching lower than the walls of his pit, hoping no one noticed.

Suddenly, he heard a voice and he dropped to the ground.

The voice was melodious, like strong music. It came from an oak near the winepress. It said: "The Lord is with you, you mighty man of valor."

Mighty man of valor. Gideon hoped it meant someone else. But he feared it meant himself. Slowly he rose to his knees and peered over the edge of the vat. Chaff stuck to his sweaty chest.

Yes, it meant him.

For there beneath the oak sat a man of regal appearance. Gazing straight back at Gideon. Smiling, seeming well contented.

Gideon, hiding all but his eyes below the stone, said, "What are you talking about?"

"Go," intoned the marvelous figure, speaking to Gideon; there was no one else in sight. "Go in this might of yours, and deliver Israel from the hand of Midian."

Gideon considered the man and the madness of his utterance.

All at once he jumped up and shouted, "Did someone tell you it was me? Well, it wasn't. I'm not the sort that dishonors his father. Besides, I'm nothing, I'm no one. Look at me: Gideon, the least of the little clan in the weakest of tribes—"

"Isn't it I who send you?" said the smiling figure. His voice had the force of mountain water. "I will be with you."

"I hated that altar," Gideon pleaded. "The face of Asherah frightens me."

"I will be with you," the voice rolled on. "And you shall smite the Midianites as one man."

Gideon swallowed and fell silent.

The two men looked at each other a while.

Then Gideon said, "I am going to bring you something to eat. Please don't leave while I am gone."

The man said, "I will stay till you return."

So Gideon went into his house and prepared a young kid and unleavened cakes. He put the meat in a basket and the broth in a pot, and brought it all to the man who sat beneath the oak.

The man said, "Lay the meat and the cakes directly on this rock."

Gideon did so.

The man said, "Now, pour the broth over them."

Gideon did.

Then the man reached with the tip of his staff and touched the food. Immediately fire shot from the rock and consumed the meat and the cakes together, and the man vanished.

"Alas!" cried Gideon. "Alas, O Lord God! I have seen the angel of the Lord face-to-face—"

But the voice of the Lord, the voice of many cataracts said, *Be at peace, Gideon. You will not die. But go. For haven't the Midianites and the Amalekites and the people of the East all come together and crossed the Jordan? Yes, and even now they are encamping in the valley of Jezreel.*

That night Gideon did not return to his house. A solitary man, he sat on the wall of his father's wine vat, staring at a pile of new fleeces which lay on the stone floor exactly where he had been threshing wheat that day.

"If you will deliver Israel by my hand," Gideon prayed, "then give me a sign. Let the fleece be wet in the morning, but all the floor around it dry."

And so it was. At sunrise Gideon wrung enough dew from the fleece to fill a bowl. But he stared at that bowl all morning long, and by the afternoon, when the wool was still moist, he was thinking that wool would naturally hold water longer than stone.

So that night he put the fleece back in the same spot.

"Don't be angry with me," Gideon prayed. "Let me make just one more trial. This time, O Lord, let the fleece be dry and all the ground around it wet with dew."

Gideon sat vigil over the pile a second night through, and in the morning the fleece was dry. All the ground around was wet with dew.

###

The spirit of the Lord came upon Gideon the son of Joash. It filled him as a body fills a garment—and Gideon sounded the horn of war, and the clan of Abiezer rose up ready to fight.

Likewise, Gideon sent messengers throughout Manasseh and Asher and Zebulun and Naphtali. Men came from all four tribes with tents and weapons to follow him.

80

This army Gideon led to the spring of Harod, somewhat south of the hill where Midian lay encamped in a valley.

That same day the Lord spoke to Gideon.

The people with you are too many, lest Israel boast in victory, said the Lord. Therefore, tell those who are afraid that they may go home.

Gideon did as the Lord said, and twenty-two thousand men went home. Ten thousand remained.

Again the Lord said, *They are still too many. They will think it was their hand that delivered them. Therefore, march your armies to the water and command them to drink.*

Gideon did so, and while the men were drinking the Lord said, *Those that put their hands in the water and lap as dogs do, count them and keep them. Those that kneel, send them home.*

Nine thousand seven hundred men had kneeled down to drink! That left only three hundred! Gideon felt as if he were back in his wine vat, helpless and small and frightened.

But the Lord said, *With three hundred will I give the Midianites into your hand. Tell the others to leave their jars and their trumpets behind and to depart before the darkness.*

That night Gideon led his small band to the ridge overlooking the valley where Midian lay encamped. Their red fires filled the dark as stars fill the heavens. They made a constant noise, like crawling insects in the night, like bees in their hive.

The Lord said, *Arise, O mighty man of valor, and go against the camp.*

Gideon said, "It is the night, Lord! No one fights in darkness."

The Lord said, *I have given the enemy into your hand.*

"O Lord! O Lord God, you have reduced us to nothing before this horde, and I am not a mighty man. I have always been afraid."

Look, then, little man, said the Lord, and in a vision Gideon became aware of a small barley cake tumbling down the hillside into the camp of Midian. It rolled toward a tent and bumped it— and the tent was knocked so hard that it turned upside down and fell flat to the ground.

You, Gideon, are that barley cake, said the Lord. Obey me now, and go.

In darkness, then, Gideon issued each of his men a

ram's horn, a hollow jar, and a torch. While they were yet close before him he whispered their orders: "Whatever I do, do likewise," he said. "When I blow my horn, blow yours exactly where you stand. Shatter your jars and light your torches and shout, *A sword for the Lord and Gideon.*"

Gideon divided the three hundred men into three companies, and sent them north and west and south of the valley, until they became a thin invisible loop in the hills surrounding Midian.

In the tents of the Midianites, one hundred and thirty-five thousand warriors slept in the assurance of their great numbers. Watch fires burned at intervals throughout the wide installation, ten thousand of those. Camels were gathered in great herds, the easier to feed—five thousand corrals, a hundred thousand head. And men stood watch around the entire perimeter, gazing out into the darkness, expecting nothing.

Then, just as guards went forth to start the middle watch, a single horn wailed in the hills west of the camp, a snarling irascible sound, as if it were a wild beast upon its prey.

The watchmen of Midian turned. *Who prowls the darkness blowing a ram's horn?*

But other horns joined their voices to the first. As if the sound were a fire, it raced left and right around the hills, violent, loud, predatory. *Who fights in the night?* Naked Midianites started to step out of their tents. *Who hazards a perfect darkness? What madness is this?*

Suddenly, from all the hills around the camp, great crashings and shatterings came down. *What? What?* cried Midian, seizing swords and spears. *What army is charging down the slopes at us?*

Now torches were exposed on high, a ring of flame encircling Midian, and human throats were bellowing: "A sword for the Lord and Gideon," and all the warriors of the Midianites were awake, now crying: *They've cut us off! Even their rear guard is swarming down the hills! Fight! Fight! Fight!*

But those whom Midian slaughtered were their brothers. Terrified by the night attack, sightless, fearing infiltration, they slew whomever came near. They killed each other. Gideon bellowed on the hillside and then watched Midian destroy itself, until there were no more than fifteen thousand left.

These fifteen thousand he pursued.

In the next days, Gideon followed them as far as

Karkor, which was their own city. They considered themselves safe. The miserable army collapsed and began to
rest—when suddenly Gideon appeared above them, even
here, throwing them again into such a whining panic that
he beat them with the edge of his own sword.

There Gideon captured two kings of the Midianites,
Zebah and Zalmunna.

The men of Israel said to Gideon, "Rule over us, you
and your son and your grandson, too. You have delivered us
from the hand of Midian. Why not continue the peace for
the generations that will come after us?"

Gideon said to them, "I will not rule over you. And my
son will not rule over you. The Lord alone rules over you."

So Midian was subdued. Neither their kings nor their
people returned to cause harm in Israel anymore. And
through all the days of Gideon thereafter, the land had rest:
forty years, a generation.

(Wangerin, *The Book of God*, 195–202)

REACT

1. At the beginning of his story, Gideon exhibits cowardly
behavior. How might such behavior be considered the antithesis of humble behavior?

2. Until the very end of the story, Gideon clings to a self-
centered cowardice. How does the Lord teach Gideon the
humility that eventually leads to courage?

3. Why was the Lord's directive to Gideon to decrease the
number of Israel's soldiers a lesson in humility for the entire
nation?

4. What lessons in humility can a servant-leader learn from the story of Gideon?

Respond

A Christian servant-leader who wishes to cultivate a humble spirit must guard against a self-centeredness that can lead to either arrogance or cowardice. The arrogant leader is so full of himself that he refuses to trust the people he leads to act responsibly and effectively; the cowardly leader is so worried that his enterprise may fail that he refuses to trust that the Lord can work mighty deeds through the most ordinary of men.

Be on the lookout this week for breakdowns in your own leadership or the leadership of others that occur because of either arrogance or cowardice. But also note the times when your own humility or the humility of another servant-leader leads to the successful fulfillment of a task or project. Be assured your servant-leader Jesus, who in the greatest act of humility suffered and died for your sins, stands always beside you—ready to guide, eager to forgive, empowering to serve.

ANSWERS AND COMMENTS

1
SERVANT-LEADERSHIP:
AN INTRODUCTION

OPENING

Pray that the Holy Spirit would strengthen and renew your faith as you study together God's Word.

READY

Read aloud this introductory section. It sets the stage for the study on leadership. Then have participants work independently to complete the exercise. Have volunteers share their responses to the questions. Answers to all of the questions will vary. Accept all responses.

The next section defines "servant-leadership." Invite volunteers to read aloud this section. Ask, "How is servant-leadership different from other forms of leadership?"

READ

Read aloud or invite volunteers to read aloud Jesus' response to a mother's request that her sons, James and John, be placed in high positions of leadership from Matthew 20:20–28.

REACT

1. The greatness of Jesus was in His suffering and death. The disciples did not understand this fact.

2. The "cup" is a symbol of God's wrath and judgment. When Jesus suffered and died on the cross He drank, or experienced, God's wrath and judgment toward sin.

3. Greatness for Jesus and His disciples was found in serving others. Jesus' leadership took the form of servanthood when He hung on the cross.

Read

Read aloud the introductory paragraph to this section. Then invite volunteers to read aloud portions of Isaiah 52:13–53:12.

React

1. Have participants circle the passages from Isaiah that reveal the loneliness and pain of the servant-leader, Jesus. Then direct participants to underline those passages that show the triumph and joy of the servant-leader.

2. We risk rejection, isolation, and persecution when we practice servant-leadership. Answers will vary. We also can anticipate joy in witnessing the power of Jesus' love in people's lives as we share the love He first demonstrated to us.

Read

Read aloud the introductory paragraph. Then invite a volunteer to read aloud Walter Wangerin Jr.'s paraphrase of John 13.

React

1. The disciples saw leadership in greatness. Jesus demonstrated leadership in His service to others. Greatness was measured in serving others selflessly.

2. Jesus attempts to teach the disciples that greatness in the Kingdom of God is found in service to others.

3. Answers will vary. We expect those measured as "great" to be served, not those who serve.

4. Jesus' greatest act of servant-leadership was His suffering and death on the cross. He who had no sin became sin, so that we could receive eternal life.

Read

In each of the passages the disciple identifies himself as a servant. These servants were leaders in the early Christian church.

Respond

Read through this section. Suggest that the participants

complete one or more of the suggested activities prior to the next time the study group meets.

Closing

Invite participants to share prayer requests. Include those requests in your closing prayer. Also, give thanks to God for the servant-leadership demonstrated to all people through the person and work of Jesus. Pray that the Holy Spirit would empower and encourage you to demonstrate servant-leadership to those with whom you come in contact.

2

Commitment
and the Servant-Leader

Opening

Pray thanking God for His total commitment to you—commitment demonstrated in the blessings He provides everyday, but most of all the commitment demonstrated to you through His Son's death and resurrection. Pray that the Holy Spirit might strengthen your faith through a study of God's Word so that you are more committed to serve God and others.

Ready

Read aloud or invite a volunteer to read aloud the opening section that introduces the concept of commitment.

Read

Read the account of John Wooden and Fred Slaughter.

React

Read aloud the quote from John Wooden's recent book, *Wooden: A Lifetime of Observations and Reflections On and Off the Court.* Then discuss the questions that follow.

1. Answers will vary.

2. Answers will vary. Ask, "Could a leader receive the same results if he demonstrated concern, compassion, and consideration for the members of his team? Why or why not?" After a few volunteers have responded, ask, "How would Wooden respond to this question?"

Read

Read aloud the quotation from Wooden about how the foundation for his leadership style was grounded in his Christian faith.

React

1. Answers will vary.

2. Answers will vary. A servant-leader centers his attention on the workers first and the task second.

Read

Read aloud or invite volunteers to read aloud the information about Tom Osborne and the quotes from his recent book, *On Solid Ground.*

React

1. Answers will vary. Allow time for volunteers to share.

2. Again, answers will vary.

3. Urge participants to develop a one-sentence guideline for the use of discipline and correction by a servant-leader.

4. Answers will vary.

Read

Read aloud the introductory paragraph. Then for the full story read 2 Chronicles 28:1–4, 16–26.

React

Ahaz rejected God and His Word. Answers will vary to the second question.

Read

Read aloud Walter Wangerin Jr.'s paraphrase of the account of Hezekiah from 2 Chronicles 29.

Read

If time permits read the account of Hezekiah's commitment to God found in 2 Chronicles 29:1–36.

React

1. Hezekiah demonstrated urgency in repairing the temple so that the people would once again worship the one true God. God speaks to us in worship. Through His Word the Holy Spirit works to strengthen our faith, enabling us to withstand the temptations of evil.

2. Hezekiah spoke God's Word to the priests and Levites. They responded to God's message of Law and Gospel by purifying the temple.

3. The success we experience as God's servant-leaders is because of Him. God enables us to experience success. We respond by praising and thanking Him.

Read

Read aloud the introduction to Stephen. Then invite volunteers to read aloud portions of Acts 6.

React

1. As servants of the Lord who served us by sending His only Son to suffer and to die on the cross for our sins, we recognize, need, and work to meet those needs, no matter how mundane the task might be. We forget ourselves and put others first.

2. Answers will vary.

Read

Read aloud the introductory paragraph. Then skim Stephen's speech to the Sanhedrin found in Acts 7:1–53. Then read aloud the account of the stoning of Stephen in Acts 7:54–60.

React

Invite a volunteer to read aloud the introductory paragraph. Then discuss the questions that follow.

1. Stephen's faith in Jesus enabled him to demonstrate persistence and commitment even as he breathed his last breath.

2. Motivated by God's love, Stephen remained faithful to witnessing his faith in Jesus even as he faced death. Motivated by His love for us, Jesus willingly faced persecution, suffering, and death to accomplish His will and purpose—to save the world from sin.

Respond

Read through the suggested activity. Urge participants to complete the activity prior to the next time the study group meets.

Closing

Invite volunteers to share prayer requests. Then close by praying for those things shared by the volunteers. Also, pray that the Holy Spirit working through God's Word will strengthen your faith in Jesus so that you might demonstrate greater commitment as a servant-leader for Jesus.

3

Winsomeness
and the Servant-Leader

Ready

Read aloud the opening paragraph that introduces the concept of winsomeness. Then discuss the second paragraph.

Read

Read aloud the introductory paragraph. Then invite a volunteer to read aloud Aesop's fable, "The Wind and the Sun."

React

1. Answers will vary.
2. Answers will vary.

3. Answers will vary.

4. Have participants evaluate the truth of the moral, "persuasion is better than force." Accept all responses.

Read

Read aloud the information about Benjamin Franklin.

React

1. Evaluate the impact of each of the statements on the participants.

2. Answers will vary.

Read

Read aloud the introductory paragraph. Then invite a volunteer to read aloud the passage from Lincoln's speech.

React

Read aloud the opening paragraph. Then discuss the questions that follow.

1. We are more apt to respond positively to a person with whom we have a relationship than a stranger. As we develop relationships with others we are more able to lead them.

2. Answers will vary.

Read

Read aloud or invite volunteers to read aloud this section. Then ask a volunteer to read aloud Viktor Frankl's quote. Spend some time discussing the truth found in the paragraph following the quote from Frankl's *Man's Search for Meaning*. Ask, "How true is the statement, 'Self-fulfillment cannot be attained when a person is focused on his own happiness, but self-fulfillment is possible only when one looks beyond one's self-centeredness and begins to serve others'? Why?" Responses will vary.

React

1. Answers will vary.
2. Answers will vary.
3. Answers will vary.
4. We find fulfillment in serving others. As we refocus our

attention away from ourselves we are able to exercise servant-leadership to others. Jesus willingly suffered and died—lost His life—for the sake of all people. Because of His act of servant-leadership, we have through faith forgiveness of sins and eternal life.

Read

Read aloud the opening paragraph. This paragraph introduces the concept of multiple intelligence identified by Dr. Howard Gardner. Select a different participant to read aloud each of the different types of intelligence. Ask participants to consider what types of intelligence they possess. Ask, "Why is it healthy to realize that all people have one or more intelligences? How does this enable us to affirm all people?"

React

Read aloud the introductory paragraph. Then discuss the questions that follow.

1. Answers will vary.

2. Answers will vary. Ask, "Why is it important to identify the talents of friends and loved ones?"

3. Answers will vary. To realize that everyone has different gifts that they can share with the group will ultimately strengthen the group.

4. Answers will vary.

Read

Read aloud the introductory paragraph concerning gifts. Then invite volunteers to read aloud 1 Corinthians 12:4–27 from the *Living Bible* paraphrase included in the Study Guide.

React

1–2. The Spirit provided the following diversity to the church: wise advice, teaching, healing, and the ability to speak in other languages. The Holy Spirit not only gives all spiritual gifts, but also unites those who possess those gifts.

3. St. Paul is trying to convey the importance of all gifts the Holy Spirit has given to the body of Christ. The body of Christ needs all of the gifts of its people in order to operate efficiently. No one gift is more important than another. As mem-

bers of the body of Christ we affirm the gifts God has given to our brothers and sisters.

4. Answers will vary.

Read

Read aloud the introductory paragraph that talks about the importance of encouragement.

React

1. Answers will vary.
2. Provide time for volunteers to share.
3. Again, provide time for sharing.
4. Encouragement energizes people, motivating them to accomplish tasks willingly.

Respond

Read through this section. Then urge participants to complete one or more of the suggested activities prior to the next time the study group meets.

Closing

Invite participants to share prayer requests. List requests on a sheet of newsprint or a chalkboard. Then pray for each of the requests.

4

Vision and the Servant-Leader

Opening

Read aloud, "But you are a chosen people, a royal priesthood, a holy nation, a people belonging to God, that you may declare the praises of Him who called you out of darkness into His wonderful light" (1 Peter 2:9).

Then pray that as people chosen by God to receive His gift of faith in Christ Jesus, you may declare the praises of Him in what you say and do.

Ready

Read aloud or invite volunteers to read aloud this introductory section. This section describes the concept of servant-leader as a visionary. Then discuss the shared vision that Moses, Abraham Lincoln, Winston Churchill, and Martin Luther King Jr. articulated for their respective communities.

Ask volunteers to share from their own experiences a visionary statement made by a leader that expressed the values shared by a community.

Read

Read aloud the introductory paragraph. Then have a volunteer read aloud Abraham Lincoln's Gettysburg Address.

React

1. Lincoln states the shared values of freedom, liberty, and equality to his listeners.

2. Lincoln asks of his listeners "that from these honored dead we take increased devotion to that cause." The cause Lincoln describes is "a new birth of freedom; and that government of the people, by the people, for the people, shall not perish from the earth."

3. Answers will vary. Invite volunteers to share possible vision statements for the 21st century.

Read

Read aloud or invite a volunteer to read aloud the introductory paragraph. Then ask participants to read silently the article entitled "Rod Grimm Succumbs to Cancer."

React

1. They treated their employees fairly and honestly. They were loved by their employees.

2. Rod Grimm and his family realized that in helping and supporting others they were making this world a better place for people to live. Ultimately, their support would provide a witness of faith to all who benefitted.

3. Christians realize that on their own they would remain forever lost in and to their sins. But God in His grace and mercy sent His only Son into this world to suffer and die for the sins of all people. We have done nothing to earn the forgiveness of sins and eternal life that Jesus won for us on the cross. Instead, God did it all for us.

Read

Read aloud or invite volunteers to read aloud the introductory paragraphs. These paragraphs set the stage for the story of Nehemiah. Invite volunteers to read aloud portions of the story of Nehemiah.

React

1. Nehemiah was respected by the king. Nehemiah's devotion gave the king the desire to fulfill that which Nehemiah requested. Ultimately, Nehemiah's faith in God encouraged, strengthened, and enabled him to make the "unreasonable" request of the king.

2. To rebuild the wall and temple of Jerusalem.

3. King Artaxerxes obviously loved and respected his trusted cupbearer.

Read

Have volunteers read aloud portions of Part II of the story of Nehemiah.

React

1. Nehemiah looks over that which he hopes to accomplish. He surveys the damage and prepares for the task he desires to accomplish.

2. God and His love for Nehemiah motivate him to carry out the plans.

Read

Read aloud Part III of the story of Nehemiah as retold by Walter Wangerin Jr.

React

1. Nehemiah gave his people tasks to complete. He ruled them with authority—authority that came from God.

2. Nehemiah shared his vision and purpose with the people of Jerusalem. The people responded to a leader. They had lacked this kind of leadership for many years.

3. God and His Word are the source of Nehemiah's visionary leadership. God's Word shared with the people through Nehemiah is the ultimate source of the people's "purpose, encouragement, and hope."

Read

Read aloud or invite volunteers to read aloud the final section of the story of Nehemiah, retold by Walter Wangerin Jr.

React

1. On the wall—the wall completed under the leadership of Nehemiah—the people give thanks to God.

2. As children of God, called to saving faith in Jesus by the power of the Holy Spirit, we "declare the praises of Him who called you out of darkness." Answers will vary to the second question.

3. Answers will vary. Reinforce the idea that all who have been called to faith in Christ Jesus have a purpose and a vision.

Respond

Urge participants to complete this suggested activity during the following week.

Closing

Reread 1 Peter 2:9. Pray that God would enable you by His Spirit's power to "declare the praises of Him" in what you say and what you do. In so doing you share a purpose and vision with others.

5
Empathy
and the Servant-Leader

Opening

Pray that the Holy Spirit working through God's Word would strengthen your faith, enabling you to demonstrate empathy to others by what you say and do.

Ready

Read aloud and discuss the opening paragraphs that describe the servant-leader as a man who demonstrates empathy. Then let volunteers describe an empathetic leader.

Read

Read aloud the opening paragraph. Then invite volunteers to read aloud the portions from *Black Like Me*.

React

1. Griffin believed it was important for him to "become a Negro" in order to understand and empathize with the African American.

2. Griffin's decision to "become a Negro" enabled him to empathize with the prejudice and discrimination experienced by African Americans. It was only as he experienced prejudice and discrimination that he could truly empathize with the plight of African Americans.

Read

Invite different volunteers to read aloud the excerpts from *Black Like Me* that describe the reaction Griffin received as a black man in the Deep South. If your study group is large you may want to divide the class into small groups or pairs and assign a different excerpt to each group. After each group has read their assigned excerpt, direct them to the questions in the React section that follows.

Rᴇᴀᴄᴛ

1. Answers will vary. Say, "Only as we walk a mile in someone else's shoes can we truly empathize." Then ask, "Do you agree or disagree with this statement?" Allow time for volunteers to share. No doubt Griffin's experiences enabled him to better empathize with the prejudice experienced by African Americans.

2. Answers will vary.

Rᴇᴀᴅ

Read aloud or invite participants to read silently the poignant story of a father and son.

Rᴇᴀᴄᴛ

1. Answers will vary. The father realized that his son's mistake was just that—a mistake.

2. The son learned that a true servant-leader empathizes with the needs of others. The father demonstrated unconditional love and forgiveness for his son.

3. Answers will vary. Invite volunteers to share experiences.

Rᴇᴀᴅ

Read aloud the opening paragraph. Then have a volunteer read aloud the story of a dead girl and a sick woman from Matthew 9:18–26.

Rᴇᴀᴄᴛ

1. Jesus' reputation as a compassionate healer caused people to flock to Him. At times people reacted in amazement at the miracles Jesus performed.

2. Answers will vary. Servant-leaders today can profoundly affect people. Words of encouragement can provide hope in times of despair. Acts of kindness can provide encouragement.

3. Jesus eagerly demonstrated compassion to many people.

He seems at times to simply move from one act of compassion to another.

Read

Read aloud the miracle of blind Bartimaeus receiving his sight from Mark 10:46–52.

React

1. A servant-leader may at times be called upon to put aside his own interests in order to demonstrate love to others.

2. Bartimaeus responded to the healing Jesus provided to him by following Jesus. Say, "We too have been healed by Jesus. Jesus went to the cross to suffer and to die for our sins. Through His death we receive by faith complete healing from sin and death. How do we respond to the miracle of healing Jesus has provided to us?"

Read

If time permits read and discuss the compassion and empathy Jesus demonstrated through the miracles listed.

Respond

Urge participants to seek others this week to whom they can demonstrate empathy.

Closing

Pray that the empathy Jesus demonstrated to you through His death on the cross might motivate and empower you to demonstrate empathy to others during the coming week.

6
Humility
and the Servant-Leader

Ready

Read aloud the introductory paragraphs. Then discuss the questions that follow. This section of the chapter will introduce the concept of humility.

Read

Read aloud the introductory paragraph. Then invite different volunteers to read aloud each of the proverbs.

React

1. Pride, when unchecked by humility, can cause a person to believe he is above the law, better than others, or is more important that others. Answers will vary.

2. A humble person considers others and their needs first. The humble person gives credit to others first, himself last. Answers will vary.

Read

Invite a different volunteer to read aloud each of the proverbs listed. Discuss the meaning of each.

React

1. Evil behavior and perverse speech adversely affect others. Pride breeds quarrels among people. Pride destroys relationships.

2. Answers will vary. Arrogance is putting yourself before others, disregarding their needs. Self-respect is a healthy concern for self-body, mind, and spirit. Self-respect does not disregard the needs and concerns of others.

Read

Invite volunteers to read aloud each of the proverbs listed and briefly describe the meaning of each.

React

1. When you put the concern for others above yourself, you gain honor and respect. Through faith we receive true honor. When God comes first in our lives, we desire to reflect His love to others.

2. We attain honor ultimately through that which God has graciously done on our behalf—He sent His only Son to suffer and die on the cross to win for us forgiveness of sins and eternal life. Empowered by God's love in Christ Jesus, we demonstrate care for others, put others first, give others credit, and so forth.

Read

Read aloud the opening paragraph. Then invite volunteers to read aloud portions of the essay on stardom.

React

1. The author sees that athletics today have become very "me" focused. Athletes are often more concerned about their own personal gain than the team's welfare.

2. The Princeton Tigers continue to demonstrate team first, players or individuals second.

3. Answers will vary.

4. An assist demonstrates your love for others. An assist puts others first.

5. Fame, the promise of wealth, and the desire to get all I can for myself ultimately affect the behavior of athletes. Ultimately, the root of this "meistic" attitude is sin.

6. The same forces that keep athletes from demonstrating humble behavior keep people in other occupations from demonstrating and practicing humble behavior.

Read

Read aloud the introductory paragraph. Then invite volunteers to read aloud the newspaper articles about the Valparaiso University basketball team.

REACT

1. The attitudes and behaviors of Valparaiso University's basketball team captured the hearts of sports fans.
2. Answers will vary.

READ

Read aloud the introductory paragraph. Then invite a volunteer to read aloud Philippians 2:1–11 from the *Living Bible* paraphrase.

REACT

1. Jesus humbled Himself by becoming a man, and then after living a perfect life, suffered and died on the cross for the sins of all people.
2. God honored Jesus by raising Him to the heights of heaven, giving Him a name above every other name ... "that at the name of Jesus every knee shall bow in heaven and on earth and under earth, and every tongue shall confess that Jesus Christ is Lord."
3. Motivated by God's love for us in Jesus we are not selfish, are humble, love one another, and demonstrate an attitude of servanthood demonstrated by Jesus' death on the cross.
4. Answers will vary.

READ

Read aloud the introductory paragraph. Then invite volunteers to read aloud the story of Gideon as told by Walter Wangerin Jr. from *The Book of God*. Since this reading is rather lengthy, you may at times want to stop the reading and discuss briefly what has been read.

REACT

1. Cowardice demonstrates a concern for self, rather than a concern for others.
2. The Lord teaches Gideon humility through a series of miraculous events. Through the event that occurred on a cross, God has taught us humility. Through Word and sacrament God continues to strengthen our faith today, enabling us to have courage as we face difficult situations. The same power God

made readily available to Gideon, He continues to make available to us today.

3. The people of Israel realized that on their own they were helpless. The decrease in the number of soldiers caused the people to rely upon God alone for the victory and gave Him the credit when the battle was won.

4. Answers will vary.

Respond

Read aloud the closing paragraphs of this lesson. Direct participants to look for opportunities to demonstrate humility as they come in contact with others during the week.

Closing

Thank God for the victory He won for you and all people through His Son's death on the cross. Pray that Jesus' love for you will empower you to demonstrate love to others—both in what you say and what you do.